Books by the Same Author

BP747	Windows 8.1 Explained
BP741	Microsoft Office 2013 Explained
BP738	Google for the Older Generation
BP735	Windows 8 Explained
BP284	Programming in QuickBASIC
BP259	A Concise Introduction to UNIX
BP258	Learning to Program in C
BP250	Programming in Fortran 77

Books Written with Phil Oliver

BP726	Microsoft Excel 2010 Explained
BP719	Microsoft Office 2010 Explained
BP718	Windows 7 Explained
BP710	An Introduction to Windows Live Essentials
BP706	An Introduction to Windows 7
BP703	An Introduction to Windows Vista
BP595	Google Explored
BP590	Microsoft Access 2007 explained
BP585	Microsoft Excel 2007 explained
BP584	Microsoft Word 2007 explained
BP583	Microsoft Office 2007 explained
BP581	Windows Vista explained
BP580	Windows Vista for Beginners
BP569	Microsoft Works 8.0 & Works Suite 2006 explained
BP563	Using Windows XP's Accessories
BP557	How Did I Do That ... in Windows XP
BP555	Using PDF Files
BP550	Advanced Guide to Windows XP
BP545	Paint Shop Pro 8 explained
BP538	Windows XP for Beginners
BP525	Controlling Windows XP the easy way
BP514	Windows XP explained
BP509	Microsoft Office XP explained
BP498	Using Visual Basic
BP341	MS-DOS explained

Windows 8.1 Explained

by

N. Kantaris

Bernard Babani (publishing) Ltd
The Grampians
Shepherds Bush Road
London W6 7NF
England

www.babanibooks.com

Please Note

Although every care has been taken with the production of this book to ensure that all information is correct at the time of writing and that any projects, designs, modifications and/or programs, etc., contained herewith, operate in a correct and safe manner and also that any components specified are normally available in Great Britain, the Publishers and Author(s) do not accept responsibility in any way for the failure (including fault in design) of any project, design, modification or program to work correctly or to cause damage to any equipment that it may be connected to or used in conjunction with, or in respect of any other damage or injury that may be so caused, nor do the Publishers accept responsibility in any way for the failure to obtain specified components.

Notice is also given that if equipment that is still under warranty is modified in any way or used or connected with home-built equipment then that warranty may be void.

British Library Cataloguing in Publication Data:

A catalogue record for this book is available from the British Library

ISBN 978 0 85934 747 1

Cover Design by Gregor Arthur

Printed and bound in Great Britain for Bernard Babani (publishing) Ltd

About this Book

Windows 8.1 Explained was written so that you can quickly explore the workings of Microsoft's Windows latest operating system, whether you prefer to use the **Tile** interface (above left) or the **Desktop** interface (above right), as many users without a touch screen PC might prefer. This book applies to; **Windows 8.1**, **8.1 Pro** and the vast majority of **Windows 8.1 Enterprise**. Also, parts of the book should be applicable to **Windows RT 8.1** that is a restricted version designed specifically for ARM Tablets. Chapters include:

- An overview of the Tile interface, Desktop, Taskbar, the Tray Notification Area, running Apps, using the Charms bar, creating User Accounts, managing Windows Settings and Personalising your PC.

- How to use the Desktop File Explorer and SkyDrive, the Internet Explorer and how to use the e-mail App.

- How to use bing maps, search for locations, services, get driving directions and help with public transport.

- How to work with and organise your digital photographs and import them from your camera, use the Media Player to store and play your music, burn CDs and install Media Center to access DVD playback facility.

- Connect to wireless networks and set up a HomeGroup, share a printer and network PCs running Windows 8.1. How to use mobility tools to keep your laptop running while away from home.

- How to use Accessibility features if you have problems using the keyboard or mouse or have poor eyesight, how to keep your PC healthy and backup your important files.

About the Author

Noel Kantaris graduated in Electrical Engineering at Bristol University and after spending three years in the Electronics Industry in London, took up a Tutorship in Physics at the University of Queensland. Research interests in Ionospheric Physics, led to the degrees of M.E. in Electronics and Ph.D. in Physics. On return to the UK, he took up a Post-Doctoral Research Fellowship in Radio Physics at the University of Leicester, and then a lecturing position in Engineering at the Camborne School of Mines, Cornwall, (part of Exeter University), where he was also the CSM Computing Manager. Lately he also served as IT Director of FFC Ltd.

Trademarks

Microsoft, **Windows**, **Windows 8.1**, **Windows 8**, **Windows 7**, **Windows Vista**, and **Windows XP** are either registered trademarks or trademarks of Microsoft Corporation.

Wi-Fi is a trademark of the Wi-Fi Alliance.

All other brand and product names used in the book are recognised as trademarks, or registered trademarks, of their respective companies.

Contents

1. **Windows 8.1 Overview**. 1

   Upgrading to Windows 8.1. 1

       Upgrading Via Windows 8. 2

       System Requirements. 3

   Internet Security. 4

   What is New in Windows 8.1. 5

   The Tile View of the Modern Interface. 10

   Turning Off Your Computer. 11

2. **The Windows Environment**. 13

   The Windows 8.1 Screens. 13

       The Taskbar and Notification Area. 15

   Running Apps. 17

       Status Buttons on the Notification Area. 19

   The Charms Bar. 20

       Shut Down Options. 20

   Creating Additional User Accounts. 21

   Personalising Your PC. 22

       Windows Themes. 23

       Selecting a Screen Saver. 24

   Changing PC Settings. 25

   Controlling Your System. 26

       Changing the Windows Display. 27

       Controlling Devices and Printers. 28

       Configuring Your Printer. 29

       Managing Print Jobs. 30

   Working with Programs. 31

       Uninstalling or Changing a Program. 31

       Running a Program as Administrator. 32

   The Help+Tips App. 33

3. The File Explorer & SkyDrive............. 35

The File Explorer and its Libraries................. 35
        Parts of a File Explorer Window............... 37
        The File Menu Bar Option.................... 40
Manipulating Windows......................... 41
        Additional Sizing Features................... 42
        The Ribbon............................... 43
Managing Library Locations...................... 45
The SkyDrive............................... 47
        Creating a Folder on SkyDrive................ 48
        Zipping Files............................. 50
        Uploading a PDF File....................... 52

4. The Internet Explorer...................... 53

        Points of Interest.......................... 54
        The Bing Search Preferences................. 54
Searching the Web............................. 55
        The Address Bar........................... 57
        Explorer Buttons.......................... 57
Desktop Internet Explorer Toolbars............... 58
        Compatibility Mode......................... 59
        The Menu Bar............................. 60
        The Command Bar.......................... 60
        The Favourites Bar......................... 61
        Managing Favourites........................ 62
        Browsing History........................... 63
        Using Web Feeds........................... 64
        Tabbed Browsing........................... 65
        Saving and Opening a Group of Tabs........... 66
        Changing your Search Engine................. 67
        Internet Explorer Help...................... 69
        Getting Help with Bing...................... 70

5. Keeping in Touch....................... 71

The E-mail App................................ 71
        Connecting to Your Server................... 71
        A Test E-mail Message...................... 73
        Replying to a Message...................... 75

Using E-mail Attachments. 75
    Receiving Attachments. 77
    Deleting Messages. 78
    Sending an E-mail to the Drafts Folder. 78
Summary of System Folders. 78
    Printing Messages. 79
The People App. 81
The Calendar App. 85

6. Bing Maps. 87
The Desktop Bing Maps Environment. 87
    Map Views. 89
    Searching for a Location. 90
    Searching for Services. 91
    Navigating the Map Area. 92
    Getting Directions. 94
    Public Transport. 96
    Printing Bing Maps. 97
    Streetside View. 98
    Sharing Maps. 101
    Traffic View. 102
The Maps App. 103

7. Photos, Videos & Music. 105
The Desktop Pictures Library. 105
    The Picture Tools. 106
    The Windows Photo Viewer. 106
    Printing Photos. 107
The Photo App. 108
Getting Photos from a Camera. 110
Scanning Photos. 112
    Using the Windows Scan Facility. 112
The Desktop Videos Library. 115
    The Video Tools. 115
The Windows Video App. 116
The Desktop Music Library. 117
    The Music Tools. 117
The Windows Music App. 118

8.   Media Player & Media Center............ 119

     The Desktop Windows Media Player.............. 119
          Searching for the Media Player............... 120
          Starting Media Player......................... 121
          Ripping from Audio CDs..................... 123
          Player View Modes.......................... 124
          Searching a Library......................... 125
     Burning CDs.................................... 126
     Windows Media Center........................... 128
          Adding and Installing Media Center............ 129
          Starting Media Center........................ 129
          DVD Playback.............................. 131
          Help and Support........................... 132

9.   Some Useful Apps..................... 133

     Health & Fitness................................ 133
     Food & Drink................................... 134
     The News App................................... 135
          News Layout............................... 135
     The Finance App................................ 137
          Company Summary.......................... 139
     The Weather App................................ 140
     The Calculator App............................. 142

10. Connectivity & Mobility................. 143

     Joining a Network.............................. 143
          Network Connection......................... 145
          Wireless Network Security.................... 146
     HomeGroup..................................... 147
          Accessing HomeGroup Computers............ 148
          Sharing Printers............................ 149
     Mobility.. 150
          Windows Mobility Center.................... 150
          Power Plans............................... 152

11. Accessibility............................ 155

The Ease of Access Center.................... 155
The Microsoft Magnifier...................... 158
Microsoft Narrator........................... 159
The On-Screen Keyboard...................... 160
The Display Options.......................... 161
The Mouse Options........................... 161

13. Looking After Your PC.................. 163

Problem Prevention........................... 164
    System Protection........................ 164
    Automatic Update......................... 165
System and Security.......................... 166
    Action Center............................ 166
    Windows Firewall......................... 167
Hard Disc Management........................ 167
    Disk Clean-up............................ 167
    Defragmenting Hard Discs................. 168
Backing Up Your Data......................... 168
    Backing Up and Restoring Files........... 168
Windows Defender............................ 169

Appendix A – Controlling Windows 8.1.... 171

Displaying the Charms Bar.................. 171
Zooming In or Out.......................... 172
Closing Running Apps....................... 172

Index 173

Author's Recommendation

It is recommended that the easiest way to get maximum benefit from this book it to have a computer running Windows 8.1 so that you can follow instructions and procedures.

1

Windows 8.1 Overview

Upgrading to Windows 8.1

There are two ways of upgrading to Windows 8.1. One method is to download it from **www.microsoft.com**, which is free, the other is to buy the upgrade media. It all depends on what version of Windows you are running at the time:

Windows 8 users are advised to download the free version from the Microsoft Web site. On the displayed Web site you'll see the link shown in Fig. 1.1 below which can be used to not only find out what is new in Windows 8.1, but also to download the free upgrade to your device.

Fig. 1.1 The Windows 8.1 Opening Screen.

Windows 8.1 Preview users have additional steps to go through. When upgrading to Windows 8.1, as only their user accounts and data are preserved – all their applications will have to be reinstalled.

Windows 7 users can purchase official Windows 8.1 media from Microsoft's online store.

Windows Vista or XP users should purchase Windows 8 media, upgrade their computers to it, then download and install the free Windows 8.1 update to their machines.

> **Note:** Users of older machines might need to also upgrade their hardware as Windows 8 and 8.1 might not run on them! In fact even users of Windows 7 might find it cheaper to purchase a new machine with Windows 8, then use the free upgrade to Windows 8.1, rather than to purchase the Windows 8.1 media.

Upgrading Via Windows 8

If your current machine runs Windows 7 Starter, Home Basic or Home Premium, you can upgrade to Windows 8 (Basic) or Windows 8 Pro. However, those on Windows 7 Professional or Windows 7 Ultimate will be able to Upgrade only to Windows 8 Pro.

In short, owners of Intel and AMD PCs, laptops or tablets with x86 or x64 processor will be able to choose between Windows 8 (Basic) and Windows 8 Pro. Windows 8 Pro offers several features including encryption, PC management, virtualisation and domain connectivity. So the choice is really made for you, particularly if you want to install Windows **Media Center** which is only available to Windows 8 Pro as a separate 'media pack'.

Windows 8 (meaning both Basic and Pro) will run all your programs that currently run on Windows 7 or Windows Vista and you can perform an in-situ upgrade retaining all your files and settings. Upgrading from Windows XP requires an entirely new (clean) installation which means that anything not backed-up will be lost!

If your computer operates under Windows 7, then it will run under Windows 8 without any problems. Windows 8 comes either as a 32-bit or a 64-bit Operating System (OS), with separate discs for the two versions. To use the 64-bit OS you will require a 64-bit computer, so be careful. If you need to find out which type of computer you have, check in the **System** section of the **Control Panel** which in Windows 7 is reached through the **Start** 🟦 button.

You will also have to decide whether to do:

- An **Upgrade** – which replaces Windows 7 (or Vista) with Windows 8 and retains all your settings, data files and programs, or

- A **Custom** installation – after backing-up your settings and data files carry out a clean install. This cures the gradual slowdown that tends to happen to most PCs over time and cleans your PC of any bugs it might have picked up from the Internet. But, the downside is that you'll have to reinstall all your programs! With Windows XP you'll have to do a clean install anyway.

Note: Whichever installation you do, it is always a good idea to backup your settings and data files before installing a new operating system. Having installed Windows 8, you are now in a position to upgrade to Windows 8.1 by downloading the free upgrade.

System Requirements

To run Windows 8 or Windows 8.1 a PC requires at least:

- A processor with a speed of 1 GHz or faster with 1 GB (gigabyte) for a 32-bit (x86) system or 2 GB for a 64-bit (x64) system of available RAM.

- A graphics card that is DirectX 9 compatible with a WDDM 1.0 or higher driver and a minimum screen resolution of 1024 x 768.

- 20 GB of available hard disc space.

- Access to the Internet to get mail or download and run Apps from Windows Apps Store.

- To use Windows Touch, you need a Tablet with an ARM processor or a monitor that supports multi-touch.

- Depending on resolution, video playback may require additional memory and advanced graphics hardware.

- HomeGroup requires a network and PCs running either Windows 8 or Windows 8.1.

Downloading and installing the Windows 8.1 free upgrade might take more than two hours (depending on the speed of your network and on the version of Windows 8 you have installed). You have about 3.5 Gb to download and the speed at which this is achieved also depends on whether or not you have disable your firewall for the period and your broadband is fast enough and stable. Then follows the installation itself with numerous checks on compatibility, gathering information, installing, 'doing more things' including a number of restarts, so be very patient!

> **Note:** If you are new to Windows 8 or 8.1 you might at first be puzzled not knowing how to configure your computer or change screens, but don't worry, all will be explained in good time! The rest of this chapter only deals with the new facilities introduced in Windows 8.1 over and above those in Windows 8 and what security is required to keep your computer safe.

Internet Security

Before you do anything else you should reinstall your anti-virus software. Without it you would be very vulnerable on the Internet. If you don't have any and you don't want to pay for this, you can download the excellent and free Windows **Defender** with its anti-virus, anti-spyware and **Firewall**.

With Windows **Defender**, your computer can be made very secure with its protection working unobtrusively in the background, but you must first sign in or create a **Live** account to get it. You need the Windows **Live** account as its password is used by Windows 8.1 whenever you start the program.

If you don't have a Windows **Live** account, go to

http://download.live.com/

to download **Live Essentials** and in the process create a **Live** password. Just follow the on-screen instructions.

Once this is done, you are ready to get your Windows **Defender** security by going to

www.windowsdefender.com

which opens the screen in Fig. 1.2 below.

Fig. 1.2 The Microsoft Safety and Security Centre.

Another free anti-virus protection can be obtained from

www.free.avg.com

but it does not include a **Firewall**. If you use this program, you must activate the Microsoft's **Defender Firewall** for full protection.

I have used each of these separately on my computers for many years and found them excellent. For more information on Windows **Defender**, please refer to Chapter 13.

What is New in Windows 8.1

Microsoft have really taken on board criticisms and concerns voiced by users against Windows 8 ever since its inception. As a result, they have produced a much better operating system with Windows 8.1 which answers many of the original concerns.

You can now use:

(1) The Start button: Tap and hold or right-click the reintroduced **Start** button, pointed to in Fig. 1.3, to open a menu of options. This makes the access to the various areas listed a lot easier to get to than in Windows 8, which should please users of Windows 7 who might now even be convinced to upgrade!

Programs and Features
Mobility Centre
Power Options
Event Viewer
System
Device Manager
Network Connections
Disk Management
Computer Management
Command Prompt
Command Prompt (Admin)

Task Manager
Control Panel
File Explorer
Search
Run

Shut down or sign out   ▶
Desktop

Fig. 1.3 The Start Menu.

(2) Apps side-by-side: While in **Tile** view, either swiping upwards or left-click the down-arrow pointed to at the bottom-left corner in Fig. 1.4. This opens the screen shown in Fig. 1.5 on the next page.

Fig. 1.4 The Tiled Apps in Windows 8.1.

Fig. 1.5 The Side-by-side Apps Screen in Windows 8.1.

Tapping or clicking the down-arrowhead pointed to at the top-left corner of the screen, displays options for organising your Apps, as shown here. After reorganising your Apps as you like, swipe downwards or click on an empty area within Fig. 1.4 to display an upwards pointing arrow at the bottom-left corner of the screen which can be used to return Windows 8.1 to the **Tile** view screen.

(3) How Windows opens: You can now select the way you like Windows 8.1 to open; either in **Tile** view or **Desktop** view. Users of tablets or touch-screen laptops might prefer the former method, while users of more traditional laptops or desktop computers might prefer the latter.

To get your computer to start with the **Desktop** screen, right-click on an empty part of the **Taskbar** to display a set of options as shown in Fig. 1.6 on the next page. Next, left-lick the **Properties** option to open the **Taskbar and Navigation properties** dialogue box, also shown in the composite screen in Fig. 1.6, with its **Navigation** tab selected.

Under the **Start screen** area of the dialogue box, click on one or more appropriate boxes to select them. If you select **Show my desktop background on Start**, this is exactly what you'll get next time you restart your laptop or PC.

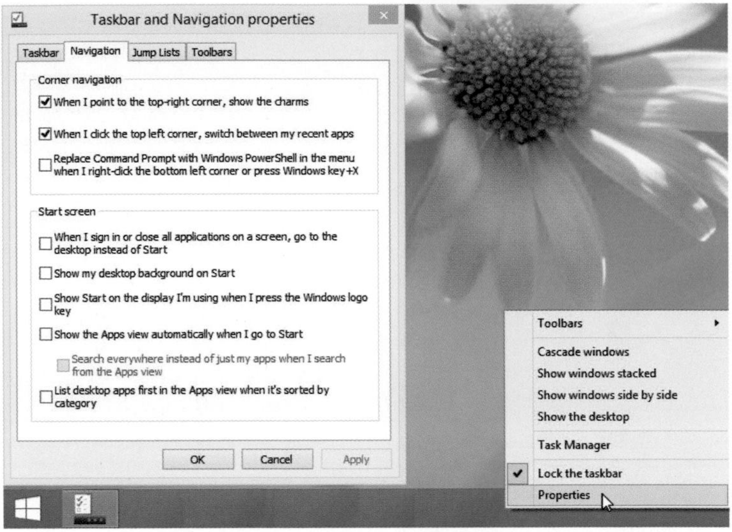

Fig. 1.6 The Taskbar and Navigation Properties Composite Screen.

(4) Searches: These are now carried out 'everywhere' (your **Libraries**, your user folder, SkyDrive or the Web). Results are not separated anymore into distinct **Apps**, **Settings** and **Files** categories.   Whether you use the **Search** charm in **Windows** or the **Search**   option from the **Start** menu, a search box is opened as shown in the composite of Fig. 1.7.

Fig. 1.7 The Search Screen in Windows 8.1.

(5) The SkyDrive Sync: The Cloud has become central to Windows 8.1 thanks to its new **Sync** engine. All your documents, photos, music, videos, settings and Apps can be stored on **SkyDrive** and made available to you anytime, anywhere. The improvements made have to do with the way this information synchronises with your tablet or computer.

You can reach **SkyDrive** by either tapping its tile in **Tile** view, as shown here, or left-clicking the **File Explorer** option in the **Start** menu (see Fig. 1.7 on previous page) and then selecting **SkyDrive** from the list under **Favourites**. The result of opening **SkyDrive** by either of these two method is shown side-by-side in Fig. 1.8.

Fig. 1.8 The Contents of SkyDrive for my PC.

> **Note:** In my case there is a warning on both screens (top-left corner and bottom-right corner in Fig. 1.8) which are the same. It reads "**Your SkyDrive is full. To buy more storage, go to PC settings**". The reason for this is that only 7 GB storage is free, after that you'll have to pay!

SkyDrive makes it a lot easier to log in to any other Windows 8.1 PC and use your Apps and documents as if they are on your own computer. In **Tile** view, enough information is used to identify a file or folder and display it as an icon as shown on the left screen in Fig. 1.8 above. Only when a file is opened it is downloaded on the spot to the PC you are using.

(6) Internet Explorer 11: Microsoft has applied its **Sync** technology to its **Internet Explorer**, now version 11. It now supports multiple tabs, placing them at the bottom of the screen when you open it in **Tile** view, as shown in Fig. 1.9 below. You can switch from one tab to another at a touch of a finger.

Fig. 1.9 Multiple Tabs in Tile View of Internet Explorer.

In **Desktop** view, multiple tabs are placed at the top of the screen just as it was in previous versions of Windows.

The Tile View of the Modern Interface

Windows 8.1 continues to support the Modern interface, first introduced in Windows 8, with live tiles. These will not only launch an application, but also have the ability to display live information such as new e-mail messages, latest news, etc.

You can group tiles as you want, make them larger or smaller and arrange them in groups such as **Mail**, **Calendar**, **Internet Explorer**, **Store**, **Maps**, **People**, **Photos**, **SkyDrive**, etc. Further along on the right you'll find tiles of the programs you have installed. Tapping or left-clicking any of these tiles, starts the appropriate App or program.

Windows 8.1 not only keeps its good looks, but I find it far more stable on my laptop than its predecessor.

Windows 8.1, just as its predecessor not only supports multi-touch screens, but also handwriting and voice, but one needs suitable hardware to use these.

Turning Off Your Computer

There are alternative methods of turning off your computer apart from using the **Settings** charm, then selecting the **Power** button.

The quickest method is to use the **Start** button when in **Desktop** view. Either touch and hold or right-click to open the **Start** menu as shown in Fig. 1.10 below.

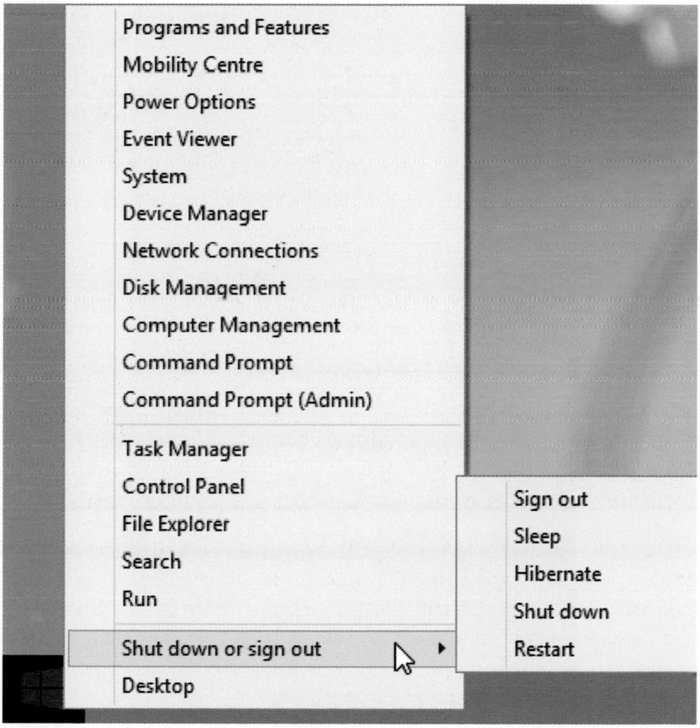

Programs and Features

Mobility Centre

Power Options

Event Viewer

System

Device Manager

Network Connections

Disk Management

Computer Management

Command Prompt

Command Prompt (Admin)

Task Manager

Control Panel

File Explorer

Search

Run

Shut down or sign out   ▶

Desktop

Sign out

Sleep

Hibernate

Shut down

Restart

Fig. 1.10 The DeskTop Start Menu.

Next, select the **Shut down or sign out** Option to display additional options to choose from.

An alternative way is to use the key combination 🪟+i where 🪟 is the Windows key on your keyboard. This jumps to the **Charms**, **Settings**, and gets you to the **Power** button immediately, as shown in Fig. 1.11. From there you can tap or click the **Power** button and select the option you need. More about this in the next chapter.

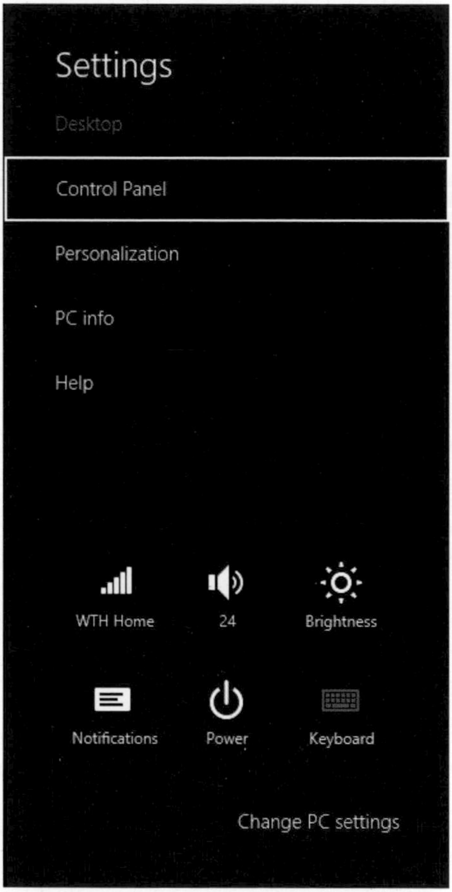

Fig. 1.11 Shortcut to Power Button.

2

The Windows Environment

The Windows 8.1 Screens

When you first switch on your tablet or PC a screen similar to that in Fig. 2.1 appears on your display, known as the **Lock** screen. Swiping upwards on the **Lock** screen or dragging the mouse pointer upwards, displays a second screen in which you enter your user details after which Windows opens with the 'Modern' interface displaying the distinctive Apps in **Tiled** view, shown for my laptop in Fig. 2.2 on the next page.

Fig. 2.1 A Windows 8.1 Lock Screen.

Note: Most swipe movements of your finger on a multi-touch screen correspond to dragging the mouse pointer on a PC. Similarly, tapping on such touch-screen devices corresponds to clicking the left mouse button. Touch and hold corresponds to a right-click of the mouse button. For more details, please refer to Appendix A.

Fig. 2.2 The Tiled Apps in Windows 8.1.

The display shown in Fig. 2.2 is the tiled **Start** screen, with tiles grouped into different sets – yours might look different. Here on the first five columns are all the pre-installed Apps to access **Mail**, **Calendar**, **Internet Explorer**, **Store**, **Maps**, **People**, **Travel**, etc., while other columns display shortcuts to other Apps and any programs you might have installed yourself or were retained after upgrading. Tapping or left-clicking any of these tiles, starts the App or program.

Tapping or clicking the **Desktop** tile shown at the bottom-left corner of the **Start** screen in Fig. 2.2 above, opens the Windows 8.1 **Desktop** shown in Fig. 2.3.

Fig. 2.3 The Windows 8.1 Desktop.

To toggle between the **Desktop** or an App screen and the **Start** screen, click the **Start** button at the bottom-left corner of the **Desktop** screen pointed to in Fig. 2.3 on the previous page and also shown in Fig. 2.4 below. Alternatively, press the **Windows** 🪟 key on the keyboard to do the same thing.

The Taskbar and Notification Area

Next to the **Start** button displayed when in **Desktop** view, is the **File Explorer** and **Internet Explorer** buttons shown separately in Fig. 2.4 below.

Fig. 2.4 The File Explorer and
Internet Explorer Buttons.

To the right of the **Taskbar** you'll find the **Notification Area**, which includes a Digital clock as shown in Fig. 2.5 below.

Fig. 2.5 The Notification Area.

Tapping or clicking the **Date/Time** display area in Fig. 2.5 above, opens the screen shown in Fig. 2.6 below and selecting the **Change date and time settings** link, displays a tabbed dialogue box in which you can change the date and time, time zone and add two additional clocks. This can be very useful if you have friends living at different time zones

Fig. 2.6 The Change Date and Time
Screen.

and want to avoid waking them up!

Below I show the display when you hover the mouse pointer over the **Date/Time** area after adding two more clocks to the local time.

If, however, you tap or left-click the **Date/Time** area now, then a similar screen to that in Fig. 2.7 will display.

Fig. 2.7 The Windows 8.1 Desktop.

With both versions of Windows (8 & 8.1), only programs that you chose to pin to the **Taskbar** appear on it, as shown in Fig. 2.8.

Fig. 2.8 Windows 8 Taskbar Pinned Program Buttons.

In this case the **Internet Explorer** button in Fig. 2.8 appears as if there are two more buttons hiding behind it. By placing a finger or the mouse pointer on it, thumbnails are displayed showing the opened **Explorer** tabs, displayed in Fig. 2.9.

Fig. 2.9 Thumbnails Showing Open Internet Explorer Tabs.

This can also happen with other running items. As you can see, there were three tabs open in **Explorer** and each is shown as a thumbnail. Moving the mouse pointer over a thumbnail temporarily displays that window full size on the screen so you can see in more detail what it contains.

At the same time, a **Close** ☒ button appears on the top-right of the thumbnail you are pointing to. Tapping or clicking a thumbnail will open the **Explorer** tab with that view active, while using the **Close** ☒ button will close that tab. **Internet Explorer** behaves the same if opened from the **Start** screen.

Running Apps

Apps you have accessed during a session continue running until you close them. To see which Apps are running, place the mouse pointer at the top-left corner of the screen (either in **Desktop** view or **Tiled** view) and slide it downwards, keeping on the left edge of the screen while doing so. This, depending on which Apps you are running, displays a screen similar to that of Fig. 2.10.

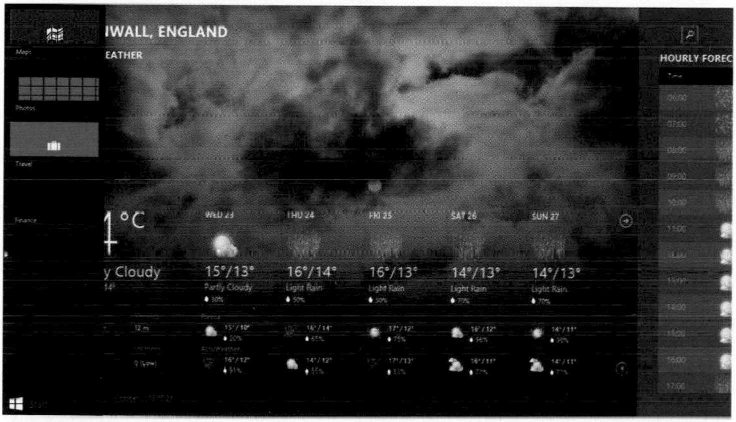

![Fig. 2.10 The Thumbnails of Running Apps showing a weather app and various app thumbnails on the left edge]

Fig. 2.10 The Thumbnails of Running Apps.

So now you can access any of these running Apps by tapping or clicking on its thumbnail. You can also force a running App to close (stop running) by right-clicking on its

thumbnail and selecting **Close** from the displayed menu, as shown here in Fig. 2.11.

Fig. 2.11 Closing an App Using a
Right-click Menu.

Another method of closing a running App is by dragging the open App from the very top of the screen towards the bottom with either the mouse or your finger, as shown in Fig. 2.12 .

Fig. 2.12 Closing an App Using a Dragging Action.

Pinned programs on the **Taskbar** can be run by just tapping or clicking on their button. To stop a running program, tap or click the **Close** ☒ button that appears on the top-right hand side of its open window or on its thumbnail, if not opened on the screen.

To pin a program on the **Taskbar** touch and hold or right-click its tile on the **Start** screen and select the **Pin to taskbar** from the displayed options at the bottom of the **Start** screen, as shown here in Fig. 2.13.

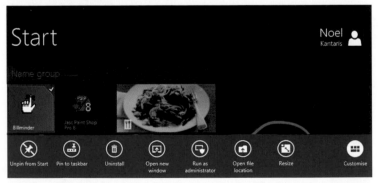

Fig. 2.13 The Right-click Options of a Running Program.

Have a close look at the available options displayed above. These differ when the selected tile is a programs or an App.

Status Buttons on the Notification Area

On the **Notification** area, also called the **System Tray**, on the right of the **Taskbar** that includes the digital clock and date, you'll find other icons showing the status of the **Action Center** ▣, power ▣ (for a laptop), network ▣ (Ethernet) or ▦ (wireless), and the volume setting of your speakers ▣. Other application icons are hidden by default and their notifications are suppressed.

When you point to an icon, an information bubble opens showing the status for that setting as shown here.

However, tapping or clicking the **Network** icon ▣, or ▦, for instance, displays more detailed information about whether you are connected and to which network, as shown in Fig. 2.14.

Try tapping or clicking the **Volume** icon ▣ to open the volume controls so you can control the loudness of your PC or laptop speakers.

Tapping or clicking the **Action Center** icon ▣ gives you a quick view of the status of your PC (Fig. 2.15).

Fig. 2.14 Available Networks.

Fig. 2.15 The Action Center.

If any problems are shown, you can tap or click the **Open Action Center** link to find out what they are and hopefully how you can solve them.

By default, Windows places any other icons in a 'hidden' area, but you can tap/click the **Show hidden icons** button ▣ to temporarily display them again as shown here. You can control which icons appear on your **System Tray** by using the **Customise** link.

The Charms Bar

Charms provide a quick and easy access to a wide range of options from either the **Start** screen or **Desktop** screen. To access these, either point with the mouse at the top-right corner of the screen or swipe from the right edge of the screen towards the left to reveal the **Charms**. As you move the mouse pointer downwards towards the **Charms**, they display within a dark bar as shown in Fig. 2.16.

The first of these is used to **Search** 'everywhere' (Apps, settings, files on your computer or the Web). The **Share** charm allows you to share content, while the **Start** displays the **Start** screen and from there toggles to the **Desktop** view. The **Devices** charm displays such peripherals as a secondary screen, while **Settings** allows you to change the settings within Windows, as well as powering off (shutting down) your PC or device.

Fig.   2.16 The Charms Bar.

Shut Down Options

When you have finished for the day, it is important to save

Fig. 2.17 Shut Down Options.

your work and 'turn off' your PC or tablet properly, both to protect your data and to save energy. With Windows 8.1 there are several options for ending the session, available from the **Power** button of the **Settings** charm as shown in Fig. 2.16 or the **Start** button as discussed in Chapter 1, page 6. The available options are; **Sleep**, **Hibernate**, **Shut down** or **Restart**.

You can select to put the computer in **Sleep** mode, **Shut Down** it down completely or **Restart** it to clear the memory settings and reset Windows.

Creating Additional User Accounts

Windows allows a whole family to share a computer, with each person having their own set-up. Each account tells Windows what files and folders the holder can access, what changes can be made to the computer and controls their personal preferences. To add a new user, use the **Search** facility from either the **Start** button (Chapter 1, page 6) or from the **Charms** bar and search for **users**. The result is a screen similar to that in Fig. 2.18.

Next, tap or click the option **Add, delete and manage other user accounts**, shown here in Fig. 2.18 as the first option to display what is shown in Fig. 2.19.

As you can see, there are other options listed in Fig. 2.18 which can help you change **User Account Settings**.

Fig. 2.18 Searching for Users.

Fig. 2.19 Managing Other Accounts.

But for the time being, tap or click the **Add an account** button in Fig. 2.19 to display the screen in Fig. 2.20 shown on the next page.

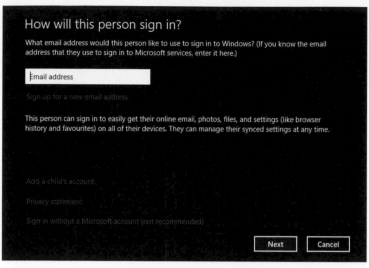

Fig. 2.20 The Add a User Screen.

Now, supply the appropriate information – it is that simple!

Personalising Your PC

You can change your PC's settings by tapping or clicking the **Settings** option in the **Charms** bar (see Fig. 2.16, page 20) in the **Start** screen to display what is shown in Fig. 2.21.

Tapping or clicking the **Personalise** option, highlighted here, displays a new screen which allows you to personalise the **Start** screen with different colours and background scenes.

Fig. 2.21 The Charms Settings
Screen via the Start Screen.

Windows Themes

If you activate the **Charms** bar from the **Desktop** and then select the **Settings** option, what displays is shown in Fig. 2.22 (only the top half of the screen is shown here) which is slightly different from that of Fig. 2.21.

Now, selecting **Personalisation** from this screen displays the Windows themes as shown in Fig. 2.23 below. Plenty to explore here! For example, you can change (please refer to the bottom of the screen in Fig. 2.23) the **Desktop Background**, **Color**, **Sounds** and choose a **Screen Saver**.   Windows comes with three default **Themes** which

Fig. 2.22 The Charms Settings Screen via the Desktop.

include most of the above changes at once, namely **Windows** (the best choice), **Earth** and **Flowers**. You can also get additional themes online.

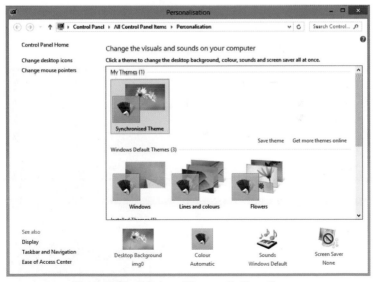

Fig. 2.23 The Windows Themes Settings Screen.

Selecting a Screen Saver

You can use the **Screen Saver** link in the **Personalization** window (Fig. 2.23) to open the screen shown in Fig. 2.24 below in which I have already chosen the **Photos** folder as my preference under **Screen saver**.

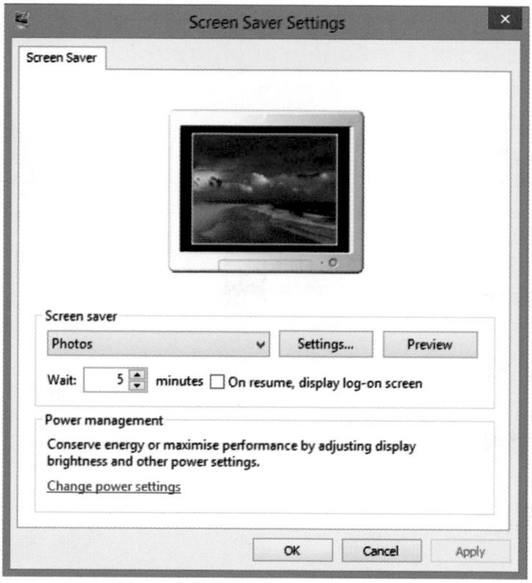

Fig. 2.24 The Screen Saver Settings Screen.

You can change this selection by tapping or clicking the down-arrow on the **Screen saver** box to reveal a drop-down menu of the installed screen savers you can choose from, but it depends on personal preferences.

In this window you can also change the time of inactivity before the screen saver starts up. With some screen savers, clicking the **Settings** button displays a box for you to control their display settings. When you make all the changes you want, tap or click the **Preview** button to see the effect of the selected options in full screen. When you are happy, stop the preview, then tap or click the **Apply** button followed by the **OK** button.

Changing PC Settings

Tapping or clicking the **Change PC settings** link appearing at the bottom of the **Settings** screen (see Fig. 2.21, page 22), displays in an **Explorer** window a screen similar to that in Fig. 2.25 below.

Fig. 2.25 The Windows 8.1 PC Settings Screen.

From here you can change the **Lock** screen (the first screen you see when you start Windows) by tapping or clicking the **Lock screen** (multicolour image above) to display alternatives or you can browse though your pictures to choose one of your own.

You can also change your **Picture password**, as well as your **Account picture**. When you select this last option you are given the opportunity to use the camera on your PC to take your picture there and then!

Do try the various listed options under the **PC Settings** before you leave this section – have a look and find out what is on offer.

Controlling Your System

The main way of controlling your PC or tablet, is through the **Control Panel** which provides quick and easy ways to change the hardware and software settings of your system. You can access the **Control Panel** either through the **Start** button menu (see Fig. 1.3, page 6) or the **Desktop**, **Settings** option of the **Charms** bar (see Fig. 2.16, page 20). Either way opens the screen shown in Fig. 2.26 below.

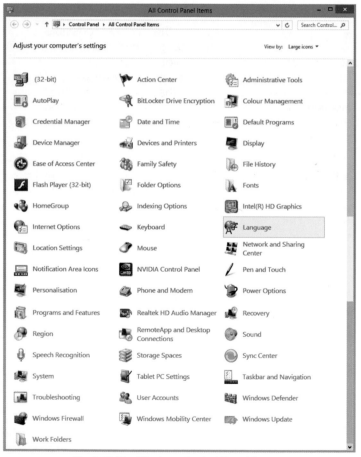

Fig. 2.26 The Windows Control Panel Screen.

From here you can add new hardware, remove or change programs, change the display type and its resolution, control your computer's setup and security, and a lot more besides. However daunting this may look, it is a very good idea to get familiar with the **Control Panel** features. Once you know your way around it, you can set up Windows just the way it suits you. The actual options available in **Control Panel** depend on your hardware and your version of Windows 8.1.

Changing the Windows Display

Windows requires the highest possible screen resolution that your graphics card is capable of delivering so that it can give you better text clarity, sharper images, and fit more items on your screen. At lower resolutions, less items fit on the screen, and images may have jagged edges. For example, a display resolution of 1024 x 768 pixels (picture elements) is low, whlle 1600 x 900 pixels or higher, is better.

Whether you can increase your screen resolution depends on the size and capability of your monitor and the type of video card installed in your PC. To find out if you can do this, use the **Display** icon in the **Control Panel** (shown above), to open the **Display** screen, then select the **Adjust resolution** link, to open the screen below.

Fig. 2.27 The Screen Resolution Box.

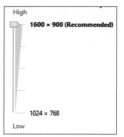

Fig. 2.28 The Windows
Display Resolution.

Tapping or clicking the down arrow to the right of the **Resolution** box, opens a drop-down box similar to the one shown in Fig. 2.28, with your monitor's resolution settings and capabilities. It is best to select the highest possible resolution available.

From the display in Fig. 2.27, you can also arrange to **Project to a second screen**, if you have a larger monitor connected to your system.

Controlling Devices and Printers

When your computer was first set up, your devices and printers should have been installed automatically. If not, select the **Devices and Printers** icon (shown above) from the **Control Panel** to open the screen shown in Fig. 2.29 below.

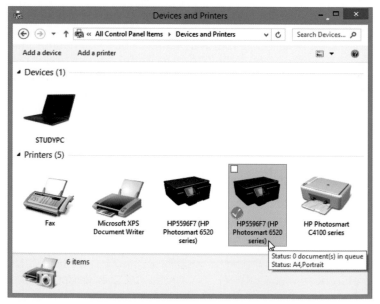

Fig. 2.29 The Devices and Printers Screen.

My **Devices and Printers** screen displays one device and five printers, one of which is a Fax. In the case of the printers, one is an air printer (the default), one for creating formatted print (Microsoft XPS) documents and two more printers, one of which is a network printer.

With Windows 8.1, most devices and printers are automatically detected at installation time, or during the boot-up process. So if you add a new printer or a new device, like a camera, to your system it should be recognised. You may be asked for the necessary driver files if they are not already in the Windows directory, but these should come on a CD, or can be found on the manufacturer's Web site.

Configuring Your Printer

To control your printer, double-tap or double-click its icon in the **Devices and Printers** screen (Fig. 2.29), to open a 'Printer Control' window like that shown in Fig. 2.30 below.

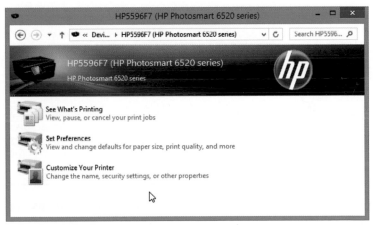

Fig. 2.30 The Printer Control Window.

From here you can control what is waiting to be printed, set preferences and customise your printer. Other device options specific to the printer might also display. In your case these will most certainly be different.

A newly installed printer is automatically set as the default printer, indicated by a green ✅ tick against it in the **Devices and Printers** screen. To change the default printer, double tap or double-click the required printer.

Once you have installed and configured your printers, the quickest way to print a simple document or file is to print using Windows itself. Locate the file that you want to print in a folder, maybe **Documents**, touch and hold or right-click it, and select **Print** from the displayed menu. Windows will print it using your default printer settings.

Managing Print Jobs

If you want to find out what is happening when you have sent documents to your printer, double-tap or double-click the **See What's Printing** option in the **Printer Control** window, or double-tap/click the printer icon 🖨 in the **Notification Area** of the **Taskbar**, to open the **Print Queue**.

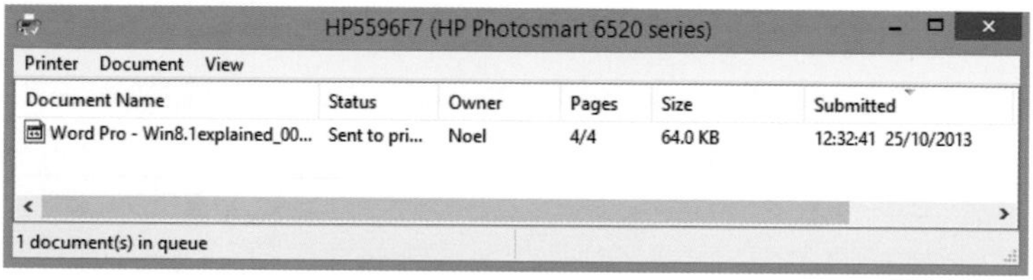

Document Name	Status	Owner	Pages	Size	Submitted
🖼 Word Pro - Win8.1explained_00...	Sent to pri...	Noel	4/4	64.0 KB	12:32:41 25/10/2013

HP5596F7 (HP Photosmart 6520 series)
Printer   Document   View
1 document(s) in queue

Fig. 2.31 The Print Queue.

This displays detailed information about the work actually being printed, or of print jobs that are waiting in the queue. This includes the name of the document, its status and 'owner', when it was added to the print queue, the printing progress and when printing was started.

You can control the printing operations from the **Printer** and **Document** menu options of the **Print Queue** window. Selecting **Printer**, **Pause Printing** will stop the operation until you make the same selection again. The **Cancel All Documents** option will remove all the print jobs from the queue, but it sometimes takes a while. If an error occurs with a print job, it will be necessary to use the **Cancel All Documents** option, before you can print anything else.

Working with Programs

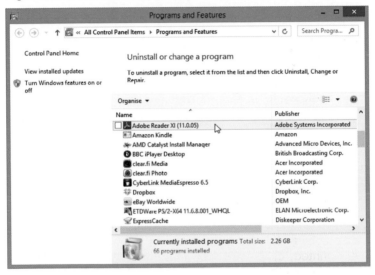

Installing programs on your computer is very easy with Windows 8.1. Just place the CD or DVD that the software came on in the appropriate drive and Windows will start the installation process automatically. If you downloaded the program from the Internet, it should run and install itself. Use the **Programs and Features** icon on the **Control Panel** (shown above) or the option on the **Start** button, to open the screen shown in Fig. 2.32. Your contents will not be the same, obviously!

Fig. 2.32 The Programs and Features screen of the Control Panel.

Uninstalling or Changing a Program

Uninstalling programs or changing an already installed one is very easy with Windows. To do either, select the program you want to work with. After selecting a program, three extra options may appear after **Organize**; namely, **Uninstall**, **Change**, and **Repair**. However, with some programs **Change** and/or **Repair** are not available, while with others **Change** is replaced by the **Repair** option only.

Using the option to **Uninstall** a program, removes all trace of it from your hard disc, although sometimes the folders are left empty on your hard drive.

> **Note:** Be careful with this application, because selecting a program on the list might remove it without further warning!

Running a Program as Administrator

If a program that you are trying to run gives you errors such as **Access Denied** or **No Permission**, then running it as an administrator can usually give the permission it needs to run properly. With Windows, an administrator is someone allowed to make changes on a computer that will affect other users. These include security settings, installing software and hardware, and being able to access all files on the computer.

Somewhat confusingly even if your account is set up as an **Administrator** you will still be prompted to give 'Administrator' rights at certain times. There is a 'Hidden Administrator' account with full powers over your computer and this is the one you sometimes have to access.

> **Note:** You should only allow a program that you trust to run as administrator as once you have given full permission, it will have complete access to your computer.

If you are doing this while logged in as a standard user instead of an administrator, then you will need to provide the administrator's password before the program will run as administrator.

The Help+Tips App

New to Windows 8.1 is the **Help+Tips** App, the tile of which is shown here. Tapping or clicking this App opens the screen in Fig. 2.33.

Fig. 2.33 The Help+Tips Screen.

There is a reasonable amount of information here and spending sometime examining it might be very useful later. Each tile, when tapped or clicked, displays information specific to either touch or mouse use.

From here, you can find out how to:

(a) Move around the **Start** screen and get more Apps using the **Store** App.
(b) Get around by switching between running Apps.
(c) Search, share, choose devices for connecting your PC to a TV or change the volume of your PC's speakers.
(d) Create a Microsoft account and store your files on SkyDrive.
(e) Use the **Settings** charm to quickly change common settings.
(f) Find out what is new in Windows 8.1.

For example, tapping or clicking the **What's new** option opens the screen below.

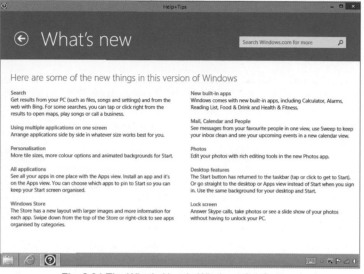

Fig. 2.34 The What's New in Windows 8.1 Screen.

You might have to open this option on your own screen to be able to read the various topics in comfort, as it is impossible to increase the letter size on this screen dump any further.

Perhaps the most powerful tool available in the **Help+Tips** App, is the ability to search for information. Using this option opens **Internet Explorer** and displays a lot more results. Try it by, say, typing **Close Apps** in the **Search** box and tapping or clicking the **Search** button. However, it pays to be brief with your search criteria, otherwise you are presented with a lot of irrelevant information!

3

The File Explorer & SkyDrive

You use the **File Explorer** (shown on the left) to explore the 
 files on your PC, while you use the
SkyDrive (shown on the right) to
save your work on a drive in the
Cloud.

The File Explorer and its Libraries

In both Windows 8.1 and its predecessor every user starts
with their own Apps, programs and a set of data folders
called simply **Documents**, **Pictures**, **Music** and **Videos**
stored in **Libraries**. To see your **Libraries**, tap or click the
File Explorer button 📁 on the **Taskbar** to open a window
similar to that in Fig. 3.1, when **This PC** is selected.

![Screenshot of the This PC window in File Explorer showing Folders: Desktop, Documents, Downloads, Music, Pictures, Videos, and Devices and drives: Acer (C:), DVD RW Drive (D...)]

Fig. 3.1 A Set of Personal Libraries.

Libraries, although not folders themselves, can point to different folders on your hard disc, or on an external drive attached to your computer. They let you quickly access files from multiple folders without moving them from their original location. For example, say you have video files on both your hard disc and on an external drive, you can now access all of your video files from the **Videos** library. How to do that will be discussed shortly.

The left pane of the **Libraries** window, called the **Navigation** pane, lists a tree-style view of your **Libraries**, while the right pane lists the folders and files in the selected location. Tapping or clicking a link in the **Navigation** pane opens its contents in the right pane.

Folders are just containers in which you can store files or other folders. Arranging files into logical groups in folders makes it easier to locate and work with them. For example in Fig. 3.2 below, folders are shown within **Documents**.

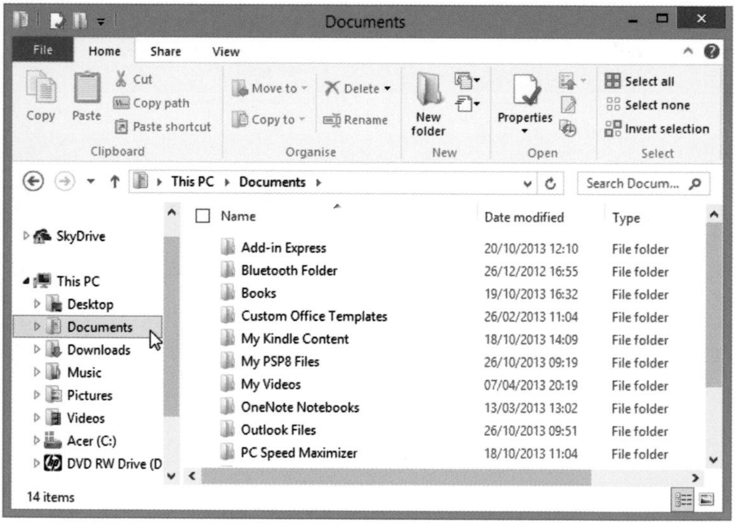

Fig. 3.2 A Set of Folders in Documents Folder.

Double-tapping or double-clicking a folder (Books in this case) opens it and displays its contents as shown in Fig. 3.3 on the next page.

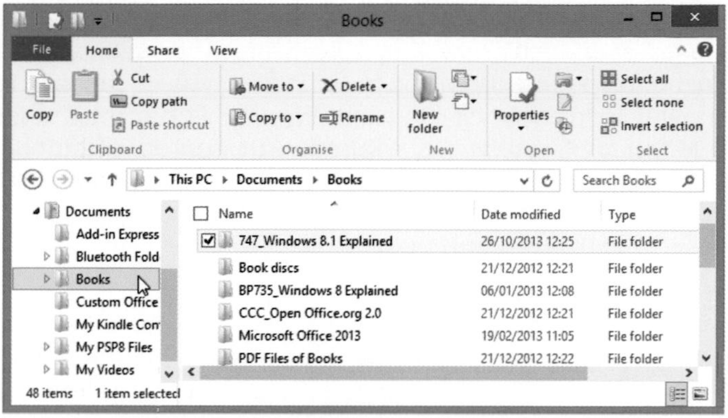

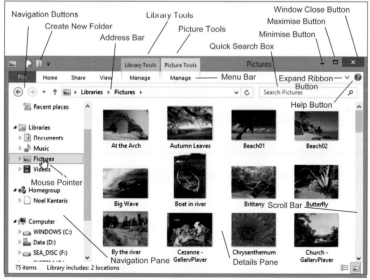

Fig. 3.3 The Contents of a Folder.

Files contain related information, such as a word-processed letter, a digital photo, a spreadsheet, a video or a music track.

Parts of a File Explorer Window

In Fig. 3.4, a typical Windows 8.1 **File Explorer** window is shown with its constituent parts labelled and later described.

Fig. 3.4 Parts of a Windows 8 File Explorer.

You may have noticed by now that the buttons on the toolbars of the different **File Explorer** windows change to reflect the type of work you can do in that type of window. For example, tapping or clicking the **Picture Tools** label above the **Menu bar**, displays a **Ribbon** with appropriate tools to **Edit** or **View** pictures, as shown in Fig. 3.5. The **Ribbon** will be discussed shortly.

Fig. 3.5 The Picture Tools Ribbon.

Once you open one **Ribbon** or used the **Expand Ribbon** ˅ button (see Fig. 3.4 for its location), then tapping or clicking each **Menu** bar option (apart from **File**), displays different but appropriate ribbons allowing you to work with the selected option. You can close the **Ribbon** by tapping or clicking the **Minimise Ribbon** ˄ button which replaces the **Expand Ribbon** ˅ button, once the ribbon has been expanded.

The typical **File Explorer** window is subdivided into several areas which have the following functions:

Area	Function
Area	*Function*
Minimise button	Tapping or clicking the **Minimise** button stores a window and its contents as an icon on the **Taskbar**. Clicking on such an icon will restore the window
Maximise button	Tapping or clicking the **Maximise** button fills the screen with the active window. When that happens, the **Maximise** button changes to a **Restore Down** button which can be used to restore the window to its former size.
Close button	The extreme top right button that you tap or click to close a window.

Navigation buttons ⓒ ⓒ ▾	The **Go Back** (left) button takes you to the previous display, while the **Go Forward** (right) button takes you to the next display. The down-arrow ▾ gives access to **Recent Locations**.
↑	Tapping or clicking this button takes you one level up towards the **Desktop**.
Address bar ▾ ► Libraries ► ▾ ✦	Shows the location of the current folder. You can change locations here, or switch to an **Internet Explorer** window by typing a Web address.
Quick search box *Search Libraries* 𝒫	The box in which you type your search criteria. As you start typing, the displayed files filter down to just the matching terms, making it much easier to find your files.
Menu bar	The bar allows you to choose from several menu options. Tapping or clicking on a menu item displays the pull-down menu associated with it.
Toolbar	A bar of icons that you tap or click to carry out some common actions (see Fig. 3.5). The icons displayed depend on the type of window.
Scroll bars/buttons	The bars/buttons at the extreme right and bottom of each window (or pane within a window) that contain a scroll box/button. Tapping or clicking on these, allows you to see parts of a document that might not be visible in that size window.
Mouse pointers 🖰 🖑	The arrow which appears when the pointer is placed over menus, scroll bars, buttons and lists or the hand that displays when pointing to a link.

The File Menu Bar Option

Tapping or clicking the **File** option on a window's menu bar, displays a screen similar to the one shown in Fig. 3.6. In this case the **Help** option was selected to show you where to find it. Each listed option under **File** displays different options in the **Details** pane.

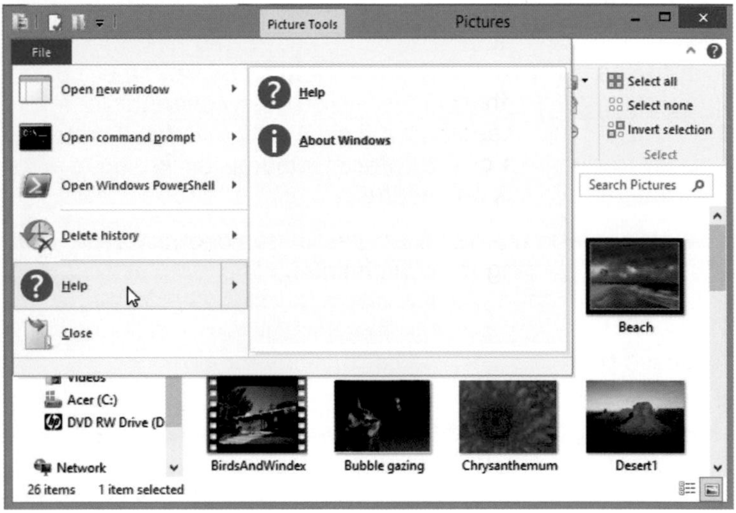

Fig. 3.6 The File Menu Option.

Items on the sub-menu marked with an arrow to their right ▶, open up additional options when selected.

> **Note:** Having activated the **File** menu, you can close it without taking any further action by simply tapping or clicking outside its window, or by pressing the **Esc** key on the keyboard. If you select the **Close** option instead, you will exit the **File Explorer** altogether.

Manipulating Windows

To use any Windows program effectively, including the **File Explorer**, you need to be able to move a window or re-size it so that you can see all of it.

Changing the active window – If you have several windows open on the screen, you can make one active by simply tapping or clicking it or, if it is not visible, tap or click its icon on the **Taskbar**. In the case of running Apps, point at the top-left corner of the screen with the mouse and slide it downwards while keeping on the left edge of the screen so that the thumbnails of the Apps display (see Fig. 2.10, page 17), then tap or click on the one you want.

Moving a window – To move a window, point to its **Title** bar with either your finger or the mouse, and drag it until it is where you want on the screen. You can only do this if the window does not occupy the full screen and it has a maximise button 🔲 visible.

Minimising and maximising windows – To minimise a window into a **Taskbar** icon, tap or click the **Minimise** button 🔲 in the upper-right corner of the window. To maximise a window so that it fills the entire screen, tap or click the **Maximise** button 🔲, or double-tap or double-click in the **Title** bar. Double-tapping/clicking again will restore it.

A window that has been minimised or maximised can be returned to its original size and position on the screen by either tapping or clicking on its **Taskbar** icon to expand it to a window, or tapping or clicking on the **Restore Down** button 🔲 of a maximised window, to reduce it to its former size.

 Re-sizing a window – To change the size of a window either place your finger on a visible edge of the window, or corner, and drag the edge or corner to the required place. With the mouse, the pointer first changes to a two-headed arrow when placed at the edge or corner, as shown here, before you can drag.

Closing a window – To close a window and save screen space and memory, tap or click the **Close** 🔲 button.

Additional Sizing Features

Windows 8.1 also includes some additional ways to manipulate windows, whether those of a program or an App. These are easier carried out using a mouse.

Maximising windows – To maximise the current program window, you drag its **Title** bar up towards the top of the screen. When the cursor touches the top of the screen, the window will maximise.

Snapping program windows to the edge of the screen – This allows the display of two windows side by side (each taking half the width of your screen, as shown in Fig. 3.7.

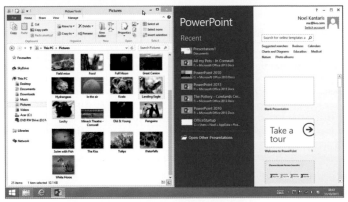

Fig. 3.7 Two Windows Displaying Side-by-side.

To achieve this, drag one window to the left by its **Title** bar. When the cursor hits the left side of the screen, the window will snap to that edge and re-size to occupy the left half of the screen. Next, drag a second window towards the right screen edge to re-size it and snap it to the right half of the screen.

To snap a running App to a screen's edge, place the mouse pointer at the top-left edge of the screen and slide it downwards to reveal the running Apps, then right-click the one you want and select **Insert Left** from the drop-down menu (see Fig. 2.11 on page 17.

Restoring a maximised or snapped window – Drag the window by its **Title** bar towards the centre of the screen.

The Ribbon

Traditional menus and toolbars in **File Explorer** have been replaced by the **Ribbon** – a device that presents commands organised into a set of tabs, as shown in Fig.3.8.

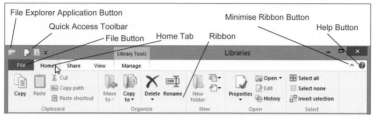

Fig. 3.8 The Home Tab of the File Explorer Ribbon.

The tabs on the **Ribbon** display the commands that are most relevant for each of the task areas in a **Library** activity (in this case), as shown above for **File Explorer**.

Note the **Minimise the Ribbon** ⌃ button which you tap or click to gain more space on your screen. It then changes to the **Expand the Ribbon** ⌄ button, which you tap or click to display the **Ribbon** again.

Also note that there are three basic components to the Ribbon, as shown in Fig. 3.9 below.

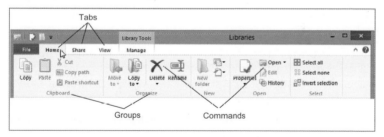

Fig. 3.9 The Components of the Ribbon.

The Ribbon Components are:

Tabs   There are several basic tabs across the top, each representing an activity area.

Groups   Each tab has several groups that show related items together.

Commands   A command can be a button or a box to read or enter information.

For each activity the **Home** tab contains all the things you use most often, such as creating a **New** folder, the **Copy** and **Delete** commands, etc. Tapping or clicking a new tab opens a new series of groups, each with its relevant command buttons. This really works very well.

Contextual tabs also appear, as we have seen earlier, when they are needed so that you can very easily find and use the commands needed for the current operation.

Below the content of the other three **Ribbon** tabs is displayed.

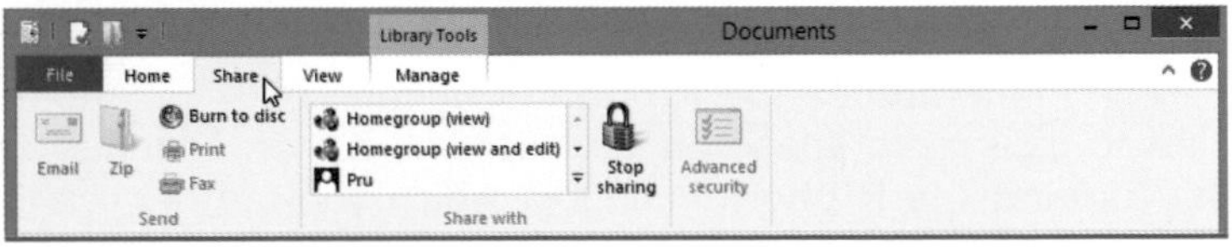

Fig. 3.10 The Share Tab of the File Explorer Ribbon.

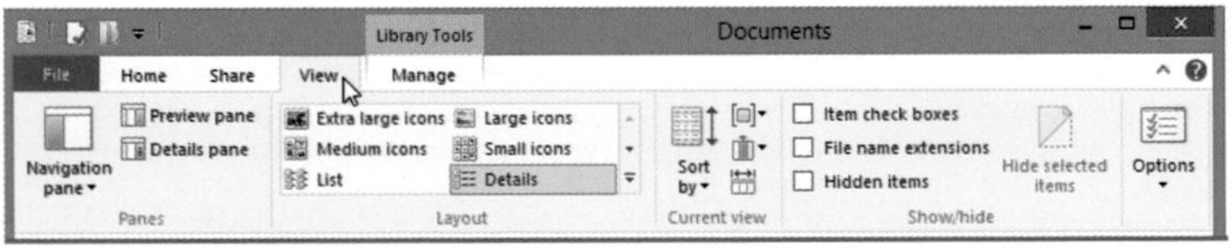

Fig. 3.11 The View Tab of the File Explorer Ribbon.

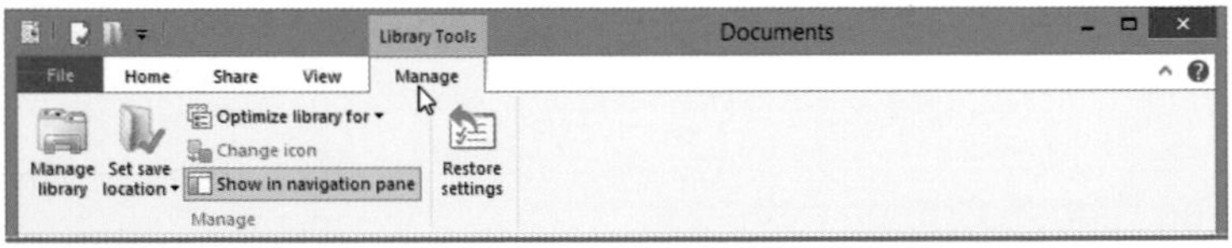

Fig. 3.12 The Manage Tab of the File Explorer Ribbon.

Managing Library Locations

To add a new location to a library, so that the contents of that location are available to the **Libraries**, tap or click on the required library entry, say the **Pictures** under **Libraries**, as an example, to open the screen shown in Fig. 3.13 below, with the **Library Tools**, **Manage** tab active.

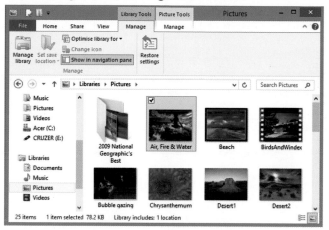

Fig. 3.13 The Manage Tab of the File Explorer Ribbon.

As you can see from the above screen, the **Pictures** library already points to a videos folder which allows it to display the above screen. To add another location to the **Pictures** library, such as a folder on another location on your hard disc

containing more videos, tap or click the **Manage library** option on the **Ribbon** (to be found under **File** in Fig. 3.13). This opens the screen shown here in Fig. 3.14.

Fig. 3.14 Adding a Pictures Library Location.

Next, tap or click the **Add** button to open the display shown in Fig. 3.15 below.

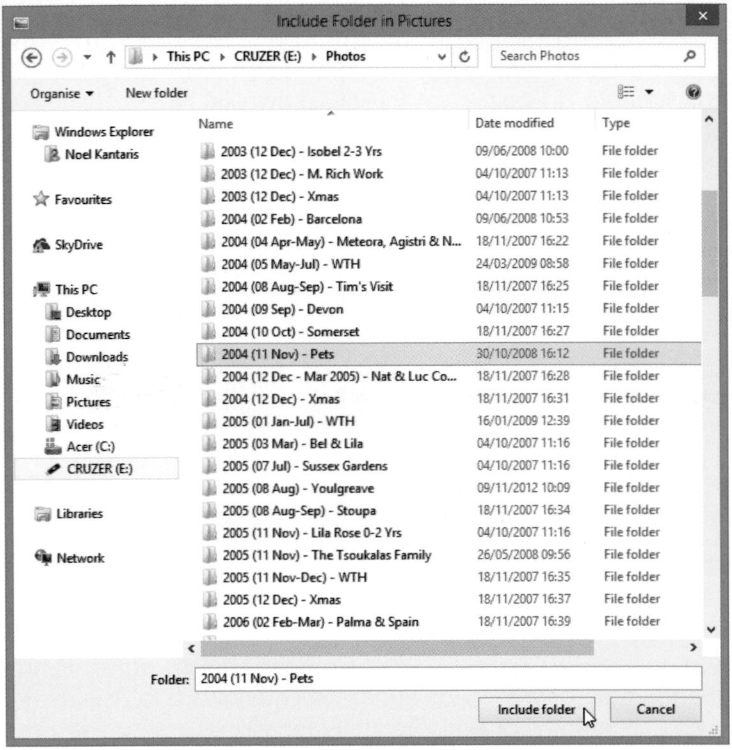

Fig. 3.15 Including a Folder from an external Drive to the Library.

On this screen you can locate the folder you want to include in your library, say a **Picture** folder either on another partition of your hard disc or additional external hard disc, as shown above, select it and tap or click on the **Include folder** button.

Do remember, however, that to access such added picture to the **Library**, the external media (hard disc or USB stick) must be connected to your computer.

You can apply this procedure to other **Libraries**, such as **Documents**, **Music** or **Videos**. This is rather neat, I think!

The SkyDrive

Microsoft's **SkyDrive** Is one of the best Web storage services available. You get 7 GB free Web space to store you photos and documents so you can access them from wherever you happen to be. You can also invite other users to access your files for sharing or editing shared documents.

> **Note:** SkyDrive should be treated as a means of sharing and accessing files when away from your computer, not as a secure place to store your only copies of photos or other work!

SkyDrive is pre-installed on Windows 8.1 and has its own tile on the **Start** menu, shown here. Tapping or clicking this tile opens a screen for you to sign in with your Microsoft account details, after which a screen similar to that in Fig. 3.16 is displayed

Fig. 3.16 The Initial SkyDrive Screen.

To view your **SkyDrive**, you are asked to go to **PC settings** on the PC you are using and sign in using your Microsoft account's details. This is necessary for security purposes. Having done so, you can now view your folders and files on **SkyDrive**.

Since I wanted to start afresh, I deleted everything from my **SkyDrive** which was transferred to it when I upgraded from Windows 8. The only folder that cannot be deleted is the **Documents** folder, as shown in Fig. 3.17 below.

Fig. 3.17 The Contents of my SkyDrive with Toolbar Active.

To display the toolbar at the bottom of the screen shown in Fig. 3.17, with relevant tool buttons to the work being carried out at the time, select the folder and either swipe upwards from the bottom of the screen or click the right mouse button.

Creating a Folder on SkyDrive

You can create additional folders or sub-folders by tapping or clicking the **New Folder** 🔲 button, which displays the box shown in Fig. 3.18, where a name can be typed for a new folder (call it **Pictures**) and create it by tapping/clicking the **Create** button.

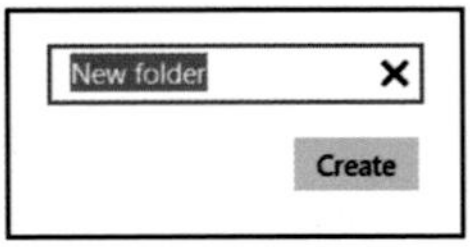

New folder   ✕

Create

Fig. 3.18 Creating a New Folder.

Once this is done, open the newly created folder, then use the **Add files** 🔘 button to automatically open all the pictures on your PC within its **Pictures** folder, as shown in Fig. 3.18. Next, either tap/click to select only the files you want to upload or tap/click **Select all** to select all of them. Finally, tap/click the **Copy to SkyDrive** button to finish the job. The result is shown in Fig. 3.19 on the next page.

Fig. 3.19 The Opened Newly Created Folder on SkyDrive.

It is important to open the folder into which you want to upload the files, otherwise they might be uploaded to a different folder! The **Copy to SkyDrive** button only appears on the toolbar after you start selecting files.

You should only save files in your **SkyDrive**, either as an additional backup or because you might want to access them when away from home.

Microsoft has Integrated **SkyDrive** even more deeply into Windows 8.1 and adds it to the **File Explorer**. The idea behind this is that you use **SkyDrive** as the place in which to hold your documents, photos, etc., and allow your PC, tablet and phone running the Windows 8.1 Modern interface to synchronise with **SkyDrive**.

What this means is that you can access your documents no matter where you are, on any of your devices. Any changes you make to a file on any of your devices is applied to your **SkyDrive** file. However, to view and change your **SkyDrive** files, you must be connected to the Internet, because the App only provides a live view of the contents of **SkyDrive**. If you are not connected to the Internet, you can only see the small percentage of these files, called 'smart files' which are held on your PC's drive. This allows you to have more local storage on your PC.

To make any folder or files accessible to you when off-line,

touch and hold or right-click the folder or files in question on the **SkyDrive** and select the **Make available offline** option from the drop-down menu, as shown in Fig. 3.20.

Zipping Files

You can use the **File Explorer** to zip files prior to uploading them to **SkyDrive**. This will help to keep you within your allocated free space on **SkyDrive**, as **Zipped** files are a lot smaller than the originals from which they were created. You do this as follows:

Fig. 3.20 A SkyDrive Folder.

- Start **File Explorer** and go to a place on your hard disc were you can select a large file to upload, as shown in the example in Fig. 3.21.

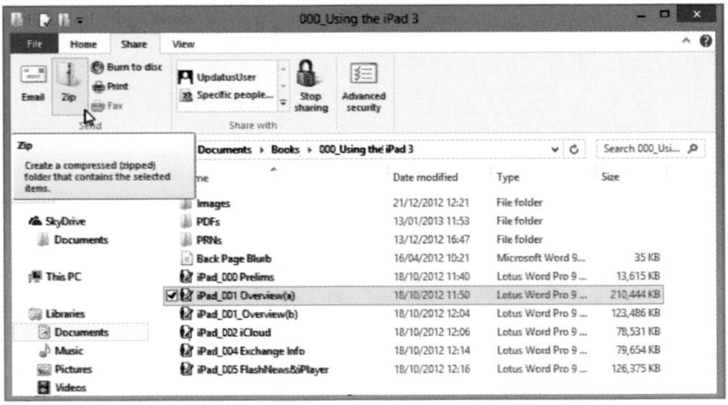

Fig. 3.21 Selecting Large Files on your PC.

- In the **Share** tab, activate the **Zip** option.

- The selected file (which is more that 210 MB in size) will be zipped in a folder using the same name.

In Fig. 3.23, you can see a drag and drop operation using the **File Explorer**. To be able to carry out this operation, you'll need to open two **File Explorer** windows as discussed next.

First, start **File Explorer** and locate **SkyDrive** on your **Folder List**, then open the **Documents** folder on your **SkyDrive**. Next, size the **Documents** window to something similar to that on the right of Fig. 3.23.

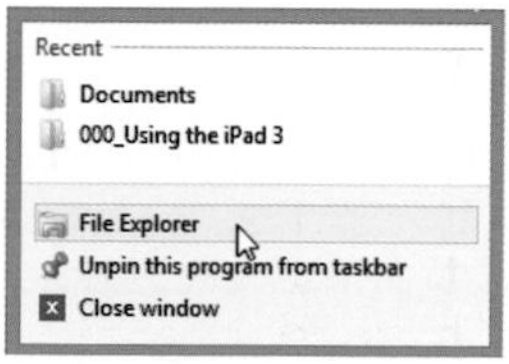

Fig. 3.22 The Right-click
File Explorer Menu.

Now, touch and hold or right-click the **File Explorer** icon on the **Task** bar and select the **File Explorer**, pointed to on the displayed menu in Fig. 3.22. This is the only way to open two **File Explorer** windows on the screen at the same time.

Next, size and move the newly opened window next to the **SkyDrive Documents** window and locate the file you want to upload on your hard disc. In this case, the 100 MB original file is zipped and compressed to just over 20 MB. Finally, drag the zipped file from the left window and drop it in the **Documents** window, as shown in Fig. 3.23 below.

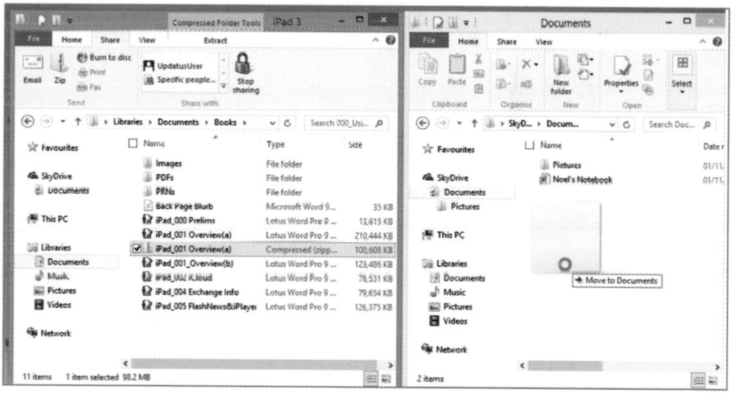

Fig. 3.23 Dragging and Dropping a Zipped File into the Documents Folder of SkyDrive.

Finally, revert to the **File Explorer** to see the zipped file in your **SkyDrive**. Tapping or clicking such a file opens it in **SkyDrive** from where you can retrieve the original file provided your PC has the program that created the original file installed.

Uploading a PDF File

If you have a very large file and you want to be able to refer to it on a mobile device, but you haven't got to edit it, then perhaps the best solution is to convert the file to PDF format and upload that version.

For example, part of a book with a total word processed file size of 730 MB, can be reduced to just under 4 MB when converted to PDF format. That size file can then be uploaded using the drag and drop desktop method described on the previous page. Taping or clicking such a file opens it for you to examine on a mobile device.

4

The Internet Explorer

To start **Internet Explorer** from the **Desktop**, tap or click its icon  on the **Taskbar**, while to start it from the Windows **Start** screen, tap or click on its tile App (see Fig. 4.1).

Either of these two actions opens the screen shown in Fig. 4.2, which displays a picture with **bing** (the Internet Search Engine) ready for you to enter your query in its search box.

Fig. 4.1 The Windows Start Screen.

Fig. 4.2 The Opening Explorer Screen.

This presumes that you haven't changed your preference of which Web site is displayed in the **Home page** of the **Internet Options** dialogue box – how to do this will be explained later on. If you have changed this, to see a **bing** opening screen, type **www.bing.com** in the **Address** bar. The picture you'll see might be different to the above, as it is time-dependent.

Points of Interest

At the bottom of the screen, which changes its image daily, there is further information on the displayed picture, weather forecast and what is popular now in the news, as shown in Fig. 4.3.

Fig. 4.3 Further Points of Interest.

The first button (top-right on the above screen dump) can be used to display the picture in 4.2 in full screen. However, while in full screen you can not see the information at the bottom of the screen as shown in Fig. 4.3 above.

The next two buttons can be used to go back to the previous day's picture or forward to the next day's picture, while the last button gives you information on the current screen.

> **Note:** There is a lot on this **Explorer** screen which you should open on your own display as it is impossible to enlarge it any further on the above screen dump.

The Bing Search Preferences

On the top-right of **bing**'s **Home** screen (see Fig. 4.2) you'll find the **Preferences** ☼ button. Tapping or clicking, displays an **Internet Explorer** screen similar to that in Fig. 4.4 on the next page.

> **Note:** What is shown here is for the **General** preferences for **bing** with other screens available for **Web**, **News** and **Worldwide**. Do look at all of these and make any changes you need to, before using the Save button to make them permanent.

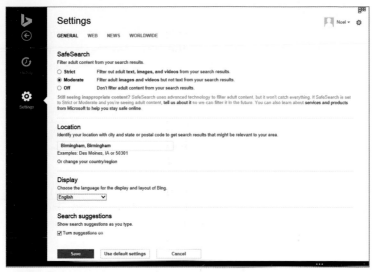

Fig. 4.4 The General Preferences Screen.

Searching the Web

In Fig. 4.5 below, an enlarged **bing** search box is displayed.

Fig. 4.5 The Bing Search Box.

Note that you can specify that the results of your search should come **Only from Unite Kingdom**, if that is what you want. However, before you type your query, have a look at the very top of the screen, shown enlarged in Fig. 4.6 below.

Fig. 4.6 The Top-left Bing Search Topics.

As you can see above, you can direct your search to specifics, such as the WEB (the default), IMAGES, VIDEOS, NEWS, etc.

To search for any type of images, first select IMAGES, then in the screen of endless UK landscapes displayed in **Internet Explorer**, type **St. Ives** in the **Search** box. The result is shown in Fig. 4.7 below.

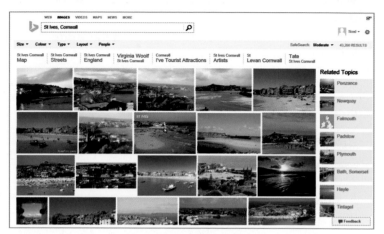

Fig. 4.7 St. Ives in Pictures.

You can also search the VIDEOS option, where you'll find some very interesting videos of St. Ives – you could almost have your holiday here and now without the bother of travel!

If you exit **Internet Explorer** by starting another App, because you wanted to, say, check your mail, then selecting the **Explorer** tile again, will returned you to the exact screen you were looking at before you left it. You will be forgiven if you thought that there is no way out of this Web page!

To exit a Website, either type a new URL (Uniform Resource Locator) of a Web page in the **Address** bar, then depending whether you accessed **Explorer** from the **Start** screen or the **Desktop**, grab the screen from the very top (the open palm of the cursor closes up in a grabbing manner) and drag it to the bottom of the screen or tap/click the **Close** button (top-right corner in Fig. 4.9 shown on the next page). These last two moves also exit the **Explorer** altogether. Next time you open **Explorer**, it will display the current (that day's choice) **bing** Web picture.

The Address Bar

There are many millions of Web pages to look at on the Web, so where do you start? In **Internet Explorer** the **Address** bar is where you type or paste, the address or URL of a Web page you want to open.

For example, typing what is displayed in the **Address** bar below, shown in Fig. 4.8, then tapping or clicking the **Go** button → will open the list of books page on my personal Web site. Note that the **Go** button then changes to the **Refresh** button ⟳ which reloads the Web page shown in the **Address** bar when it is tapped or clicked.

http://www.kantaris.com/noel/list.htm

Fig. 4.8 The Address Bar.

The **Address** bar is the main way of opening new Web pages when you know their URLs. A drop-down menu of the most recent locations you have entered, can be opened by tapping or clicking the arrowhead, the **Autocomplete** ▼ button, at the right of the address box when available.

Explorer Buttons

The **Internet Explorer** (when opened from the **Desktop**) is fully equipped with toolbars, which have buttons you can tap or click to quickly carry out a program function, as shown below in Fig. 4.9.

Fig. 4.9 The Internet Explorer Address Bar and Buttons.

It is possible to add several toolbars to the above display by touching and holding or right-clicking on an empty part on the top blue band of the above screen to display a drop-down menu of **Toolbar** options (see Fig. 4.10 on the next page).

Desktop Internet Explorer Toolbars

You can choose which toolbars to display by tapping or clicking the ones you want to see. This places a tick mark against the selected toolbar. Tapping or clicking again a selected toolbar, deselects it.

Fig. 4.11 shows what you'll see if all the toolbars on the list were to be selected.

Fig. 4.10 The Toolbars List.

Fig. 4.11 Displaying All the Toolbars.

Tapping or clicking the down-arrowhead at the extreme right of the **Status** bar (at the bottom of Fig. 4.11), opens a menu of **Zoom** options, as shown here in Fig. 4.12.

Fig. 4.12 Zoom Options.

Most of the buttons on the **Address** bar and other toolbars are pretty self-explanatory. Those on the **Address** bar have the following functions:

Button		*Function*
⬅	**Back**	Displays the previous page viewed. If there isn't one this is 'greyed out'.
➡	**Forward**	Displays the next page on the **History** list.
▾	**Autocomplete**	Opens a drop-down menu of the autocomplete address bar pages.
🖼	**Compatibility**	Improves the display of Web sites designed for an older browser.
↻	**Refresh**	Brings a fresh copy of the current Web page to the viewer.
✕	**Stop**	Halts any on-line transfer of data.
🔎	**Search**	Searches for the text typed into the **Search** box.

Compatibility Mode

You may find that **Internet Explorer 11** does not render some older Web pages correctly. One of my online banking sites for example has some problems with pagination. To resolve these types of problem, just tap or click the **Compatibility View** 🖼 button at the right end of the **Address** bar. This displays the Web site as it would be if viewed in a previous version of **Internet Explorer**, and usually corrects display problems like misaligned text, images, or text boxes.

This only affects the Web site that was active when you select the **Compatibility View** button, other sites open at the same time will still use normal **Explorer** functionality.

The **Compatibility View** 🖼 button only seems to appear on the **Address** bar when it may be needed, so as time goes by and Web developers bring their sites up to 'scratch' you probably won't see it very often!

The Menu Bar

The **Menu** bar is located below the **Address** bar (see Fig. 4.13). It displays sub-menus when one of its menu options (**File**, **Edit**, **View**, **Favourites**, **Tools** or **Help**) is selected. Fig. 4.13 shows the sub-menu of **Help** and what displays if you select the **About Internet Explorer** option.

Fig. 4.13 The Internet Options Dialogue Box.

Most of the **Menu** bar options are fairly self-explanatory, so I leave you to investigate them by yourself. The only option that merits deliberation in some detail is **Favourites**, to be discussed shortly.

The Command Bar

The **Command** bar, below the **Menu** toolbar (see Fig. 4.13), has the following default buttons:

Button		*Function*
🏠	**Home**	Displays your specified home page, with a Microsoft page as the default.
📰	**Feeds**	View Feeds on the open Web site. If a feed is not detected the colour of the icon remains grey.
✉	**Read Mail**	Opens your mail client so that you can read your e-mail messages.

Print	Prints the open Web page, or frame, using the current print settings.
Page ▾	Opens a menu that allows you to open a new window, save the current page, send it or a link to send it by e-mail to a recipient, zoom the page, or change the text size on it.
Safety ▾	Displays a drop-down menu that allows you to delete the browsing **History**, browse in private, see the privacy policy of Web pages, turn on the **SmartScreen Filter** so that unsafe Web sites can be reported, and activate **Windows Update**.
Tools ▾	Displays a drop-down menu that allows you to diagnose connection problems, reopen the last browsing session, manage pop-ups, specify your Internet options, and generally control how **Explorer** works.
❓▾	Opens a drop-down menu giving quick access to **Help** topics.

The Favourites Bar

The **Favourites** bar has the following buttons:

Button	*Function*
Favourites	Opens the **Favourites Center** from which you can choose the **Favourites**, **Feeds** or **History** bars.
Add to	Adds a favourite site to the **Favourites** bar.

In addition, there are links to suggested Microsoft Web sites.

Managing Favourites

Using **Favourites** (Bookmarks), is an easy way to save Web page addresses for future use. It's much easier to select a

Fig. 4.14 Favourites Centre.

page from a sorted list, than to manually type a URL address into the **Address** field. You don't have to remember the address and are less likely to make a typing error!

With **Internet Explorer** your **Favourites** are kept in the **Favourites Center**, shown in Fig. 4.14, opened by tapping or clicking the **Open Favourites Center** button.

To keep the list open in a separate pane, tap/click the **Pin the Favourites Center** button. To unpin it, tap/click its **Close** button.

Adding a Favourite – There are several ways to add a **Favourite** to your list:

One way is to tap or click the **Add to Favourites** button to add the address of the Web page you are viewing to a **Favourites** bar which displays to the right of the **Add to Favourites** button. Another way is to touch and hold or right-click the Web page you are viewing and select **Add to Favourites** from the drop-down menu. This opens the **Add a Favourite** dialogue box (Fig. 4.15) in which you can give the new **Favourite** a name, and choose a folder to put it in. Then just tap or click the **Add** button to finish.

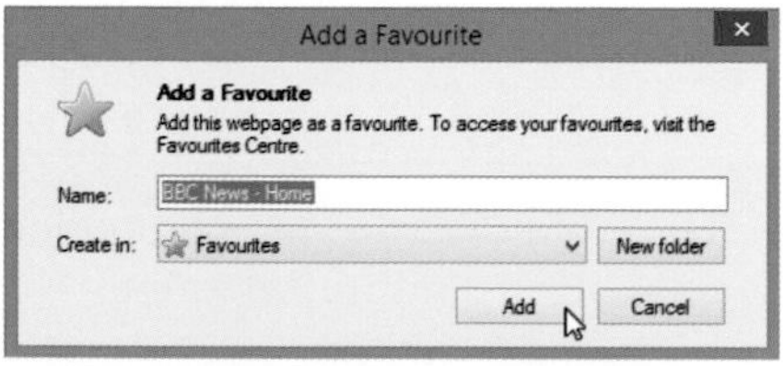

Fig. 4.15 The Add a Favourite Box.

Browsing History

Internet Explorer stores details of all the Web pages and files you view on your hard disc, and places temporary pointers to them in a folder. To return to these in the future, tap or click the **View History** tab in the **Favourites Centre**, to open the **History** list shown in Fig. 4.16.

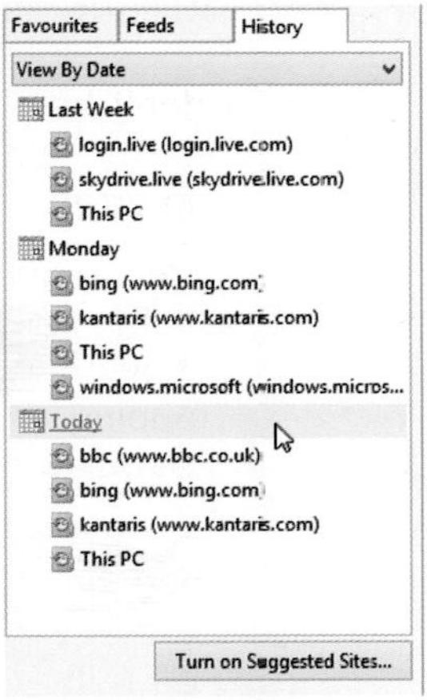

Fig. 4.16 Web Browsing History.

In this list you can see what Web sites you visited in the last 3 weeks. Tapping or clicking a listed site opens links to the individual Web pages you went to. Selecting any of these will open the page again.

The length of time history items are kept on your hard disc can be set by using the **Tools** button and selecting **Internet Options** to open the tabbed dialogue box shown in Fig. 4.17.

Tapping or clicking the **Settings** button in the **Browsing history** section, pointed to here, opens an additional dialogue box in which you can select the number of days that **History** files are kept (between 0 and 999) in the **History** tab. To delete all history items click the **Delete** button in the **Internet Options** box, which will release the hard disc space used.

Fig. 4.17 General Internet Options.

Using Web Feeds

Web feeds (feeds for short) are usually used for news and blogs and contain frequently updated content published by a Web site. You can use feeds if you want updates to a Web site to be automatically downloaded to your PC.

When you visit a Web page that contains feeds, the grey **Feeds** button on the Internet Explorer toolbar changes to orange. To look at the feeds, click the feed symbol. To get content automatically downloaded to your computer, you will need to subscribe to the feed. This is very easy to do, and doesn't cost anything! Just tapping or clicking a **Subscribe to this feed** link, like that shown in Fig. 4.18, opens the **Subscribe to this Feed** box shown in Fig. 4.19.

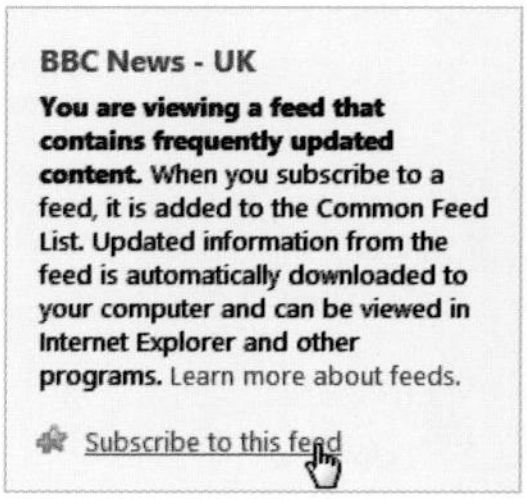

> **BBC News - UK**
> **You are viewing a feed that contains frequently updated content.** When you subscribe to a feed, it is added to the Common Feed List. Updated information from the feed is automatically downloaded to your computer and can be viewed in Internet Explorer and other programs. Learn more about feeds.
> 🐾 Subscribe to this feed

Fig. 4.18 Subscribing to a Web Feed.

Fig. 4.19 Subscribe to this Feed Box.

Clicking the **Subscribe** button adds the feed to the 'Common Feed List' in the **Favourites Centre**, and updated information from the feed will be automatically downloaded to your computer for viewing in **Internet Explorer**.

All your subscribed feeds will be listed in the **Feeds** section of the **Favourites Centre**. Selecting an item in the **Feeds** list, shown in Fig. 4.20, will open it in the main **Explorer** pane so you can keep up to date.

Fig. 4.20 Feeds List.

Tabbed Browsing

With tabbed browsing you can open several Web sites in one **Explorer** window each in its own tab, and switch between them by clicking on their tab. To create a new tab, tap or click the **New Tab** icon 🔲, pointed to in Fig. 4.21, immediately to the right of the existing tabs.

Fig. 4.21 Creating a New Tab.

Selecting the **New tab** icon, displays the address you chose for your **Home** page (**bing** in this case) which you'll have to replace with a new address.

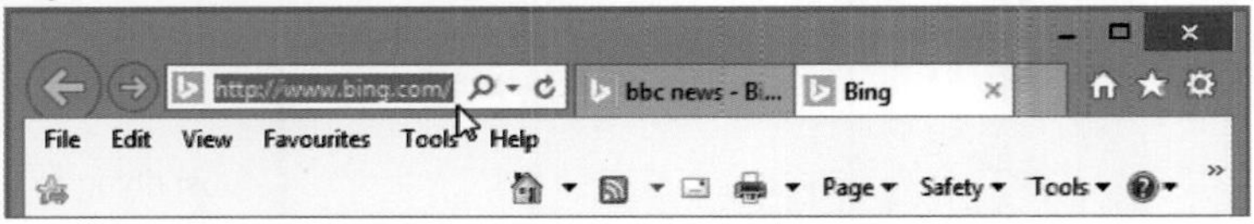

Fig. 4.22 The New Bing Page Tab.

The entry in the **Address** bar is already select for you, so simply type a new Web address or use the **Favourites** 🌟 button or select **Favourites** from the **Menu** bar and open one of your **Favourites**.

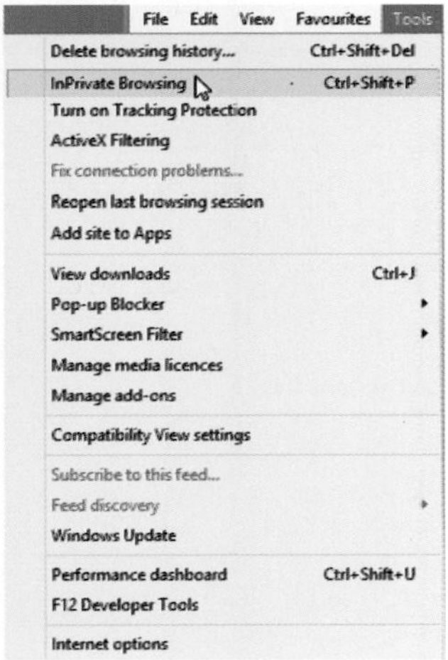

Explorer 11 retains the **InPrivate Browsing** mode of its predecessor which is opened by selecting **Tools** in the **Menu** bar, as shown in Fig. 4.23. This opens a new window with information about the **InPrivate** mode and also informs you that it has been turned on. You can now safely browse without leaving any traces. Just closing the **InPrivate** window returns you to standard mode

Fig. 4.23 The Tools Menu Bar Options.

Saving and Opening a Group of Tabs

To save a group of tabs so that you can open the pages again, do the following: Open the Web sites you want to save, maybe ones with a common theme. Tap or click the **Favourites** ⭐ button to open the **Favourites Center**, then click the down-arrow ▾ button by the **Add to Favourites** box, and select **Add Current Tabs to Favourites** from the drop-down list.

In the displayed dialogue box give a name to the folder to contain the selected Web sites – I called it **Best Buys**, (Fig. 4.24) and click the **Add** button.

Fig. 4.24 The Add Tabs to Favourites Box.

To open a group of tabs, click the **Favourites** ⭐ button, select the group folder you want to open (see Fig. 4.25), and either click the arrow to the right of the folder name ➡ to open all the tabbed sites in the group, or tap/click the folder to display all the Web sites in it and select one of them.

Fig. 4.25 Opening a Group of Tabs.

Changing Your Search Engine

You could change which Internet search engine you are using, if you are not happy with **bing**. For example, to change to **Google**, type **www.google.co.uk** in the **Address** bar (see Fig. 4.26) and either press the **Enter** key on the keyboard or tap/click the **Go to** → button to the right of the **Address** bar to open **Google**'s UK search page, as shown below.

Fig. 4.26 The Google Internet Browser.

To make **Google** your default search engine, click the **Tools** ⚙ icon (pointed to at the top-right corner in Fig. 4.27), to open the **Tools** menu shown here. Next, tap or click the **Internet options** entry (also pointed to in Fig. 4.27), to open the multi-tab dialogue box shown in Fig. 4.28 on the next page.

Fig. 4.27 The Tools Menu.

Fig. 4.28 The Internet Options Dialogue Box.

All you have to do now is replace the entry in the **Home page** text box with **www.google.co.uk/** and click the **Use current** button, followed by the **OK** button. From now on, whenever you tap or click on the **Internet Explorer** icon or tile, you will be displaying the **Google** UK page.

> **Note:** As this book is about Microsoft's Windows 8.1, I'll continue with what is supplied with it. Therefore, in what follows the **bing** search engine will be used.

Internet Explorer Help

You can get help with **Explorer** by tapping or clicking the **Help** 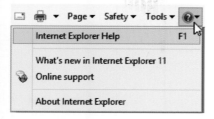 button at the extreme right of the **Toolbar** and selecting the **Internet Explorer Help** entry from the drop-down menu of options shown in Fig. 4.29.

▭ 🖶 ▾	Page ▾	Safety ▾	Tools ▾	❷▾

Internet Explorer Help	F1
What's new in Internet Explorer 11	
🌐 Online support	
About Internet Explorer	

Fig. 4.29 Getting Help with Internet Explorer.

This displays the **Internet Explorer Help** screen shown in Fig. 4.30 below.

Windows

Internet Explorer

Top Solutions   Get started with Internet Explorer

Troubleshoot problems   Making Internet Explorer your default browser

Make Internet Explorer easier to use

Download and print

Security and privacy

Adding to, viewing and organising favourites

Change your home page

Delete cookies

Install Java in Internet Explorer

Navigate with tabs

Reopen or restore a browsing session

Fig. 4.30 The Internet Explorer Help Screen.

You can work your way through the items listed on the left of the screen at your leisure. As you tap or click each such item, it opens a screen of links appropriate to that option. What is displayed first under **Top Solutions** is the **Get Started** link.

Getting Help with Bing

You can get help with **bing** by activating the **Help** entry at the bottom of a **Bing** screen, pointed to in Fig. 4.31 below.

Fig. 4.31 The Bing Help Link.

This opens the **Bing Help** screen shown in Fig. 4.32 below which lists several help topics and also has the facility to search for a particular topic.

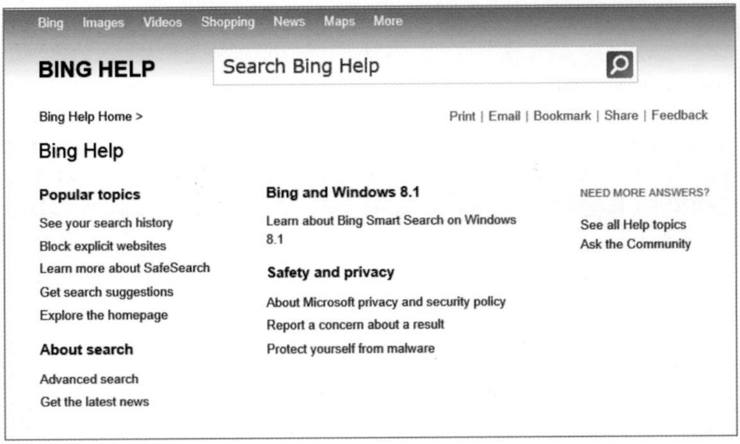

Fig. 4.32 The Bing Help Screen.

Perhaps you could get back to this screen when you need help with some topic.

5

Keeping in Touch

The E-mail App

Windows 8.1 comes with a revamped **Mail** App, the tile which is to be found at the top-left corner of the **Start** screen. It is a similar program to the one in Windows **Live Essentials**. The App is designed to work with Windows 8.1 and as long as you are connected to the Internet and set up correctly, you can communicate with others by e-mail wherever they are in the world, all you need to know is their e-mail address. In this chapter I look at Windows **Mail**, but you can also use another program if you prefer.

Connecting to Your Server

If you already have a **Live** mail account, then the **Mail** App will detect it, if not, then when you start **Mail** for the first time, you will be prompted to add one. You will need the following information from the supplier of your e-mail service:

- Your e-mail address and password

- The type of e-mail server to be used

- The address of the incoming and outgoing e-mail servers you should use.

If the connection process does not start automatically, use the **Settings** charm, pointed to in Fig. 5.1, to display the **Settings** screen, the top-half of which is shown in Fig. 5.2 on the next page.

Fig. 5.1 The Settings Charm.

Fig. 5.2 The Settings Menu.

Next, select the **Accounts** option pointed to in Fig. 5.2, to display Fig. 5.3. Activating the **Add an account** option, displays the screen shown in Fig. 5.4.

Fig. 5.3 Adding an Account.

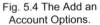

Fig. 5.4 The Add an Account Options.

As you can see in Fig. 5.4, you have a number of choices of Internet-based accounts, but if you have an Internet-based account that is not listed or you need to add an account based on a Website, then you can choose the **Other account** option.

You can add all your different e-mail accounts by following the same procedure so you can view them all from the same window. Once your connection is established, opening the **Inbox** will display any messages waiting in your mailbox, as shown in Fig. 5.5 on the next page with a displayed e-mail already opened.

This shows the layout of the Windows **Mail** screen with the e-mail I sent to myself on the third pane. The three panes are; the **Folder** pane on the left, a **Message List** in the centre and a **Reading** pane on the right.

To see all your mail folders, tap or click the **Folder** option in the first pane. The displayed list contains folders, such as **Inbox**, **Drafts**, **Sent items**, **Outbox**, etc. Tapping or clicking one of these, displays its contents in the **Message List**. Selecting a message in the list, opens it in the **Reading** pane.

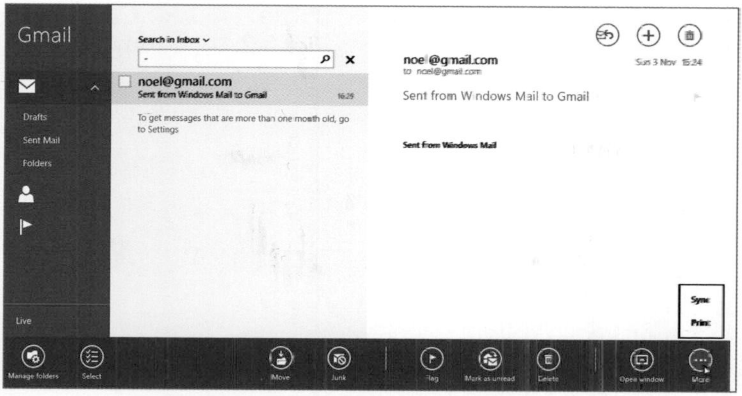

Fig. 5.5 The Windows Mail Screen.

In the above screen, additional tools are displayed which can be revealed by either swiping upwards from the bottom of the screen or right-clicking with the mouse. Tapping or clicking the **More** button displays a pop-up menu with **Sync** and **Print**, options, as shown at the bottom-right corner of the screen.

A Test E-mail Message

Before explaining in more detail other features of Windows **Mail**, I will step through the procedure of sending a very simple e-mail message. The best way to test out any unfamiliar e-mail features is to send a test message to your own e-mail address. This saves wasting somebody else's time, and the message can be checked very quickly. In fact, this is what was done above.

To start, touch or click the **New** ⊕ button at the top-right corner of the screen shown in Fig. 5.5 to open the **New Message** window, shown in Fig. 5.6 on the next page.

Type your own e-mail address in the **To** field, and a title for the message in the **Add a subject** field which will form a header for the message when it is received, so it helps to show in a few words what the message is about.

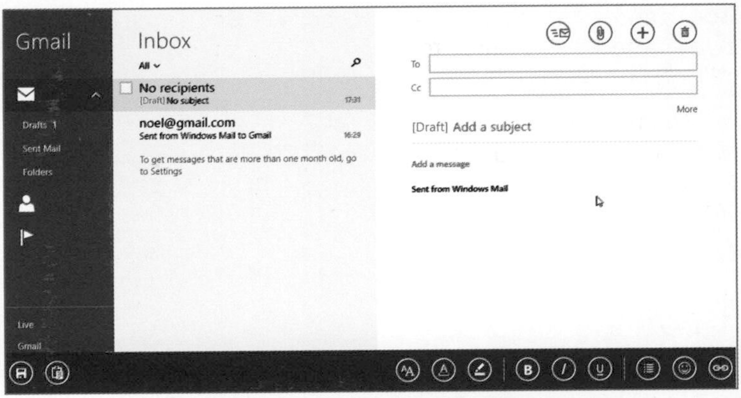

Fig. 5.6 Sending a Test Message.

Next, type your own text in the **Add a message** field as shown above. Note that to display the bar of tools at the bottom of the screen which allow you to enhance your text, change its colour, increase its font size and much more, either swipe from the bottom of the screen upwards or click the right mouse button. If you make mistakes and want to delete the message, press the **Delete** ⊙ button otherwise press the **Send** ⊕ button (top right of screen).

By default, your message is placed in the **Outbox** folder and sent immediately if you are on Broadband. When **Mail** next checks for mail, it should find the message and download it into your **Inbox** folder.

> **Note:** A **Bcc** field and **Priority** (see next page for explanation) only display when you tap or click the **More** button which is to be found just below the **Cc** field.

Cc in Fig. 5.6 stands for 'carbon copy'. Anyone listed in the **Cc** field of a message receives a copy of that message when you send it. All other recipients of that message can see that the person you designated as a **Cc** recipient received a copy of the message.

Bcc stands for 'blind carbon copy'. **Bcc** recipients are invisible to all the other recipients of the message (including other **Bcc** recipients).

Tapping or clicking the down arrow against **Priority**, displays the available options as shown in Fig. 5.7. You can change the priority if you need to, but the default is normally good enough.

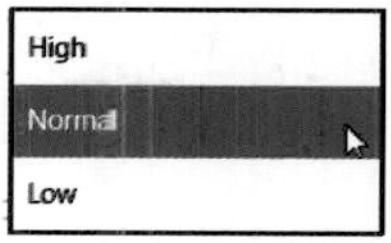

High
Normal
Low

Fig. 5.7 Priority Options.

Replying to a Message

When you receive an e-mail message that you want to reply to, **Mail** makes it very easy to do. The reply address and the new message subject fields are both added automatically for you. Also, by default, the original message is quoted in the reply window for you to edit as required.

With the message you want to reply to still open, tap or click the **Respond** ⤺ button to display the available options, shown in Fig. 5.8. As you can see, you can **Reply** only to the person who sent you the message, or to all the people who received the message. The **Forward** option is used to forward the message to another person altogether, in which case you'll have to supply their e-mail address.

Reply
Reply all
Forward

Fig. 5.8.

Using E-mail Attachments

To add an attachment to an e-mail message, such as a photo or work file, simply tap or click the **Attach** ▬ button to be found at the top-right of the screen when you are composing an e-mail. Doing so displays what is shown in Fig. 5.9 on the next page.

Mail assumes that you are about to attach a picture, so it displays all the photos in your **Pictures** library. However, you can tap or click the down-arrowhead against **Libraries**, to open a set of alternative options, such as **SkyDrive**, **This PC**, **Libraries**, etc., including the **Sound Recorder** to record a message. These are also shown open in Fig. 5.9.

Fig. 5.9 Selecting Items to Attach to a Message.

Having selected, say some photos you want to attach, tap or click the **Attach** button to complete the process. Your e-mail should now look similar to the one shown in Fig. 5.10.

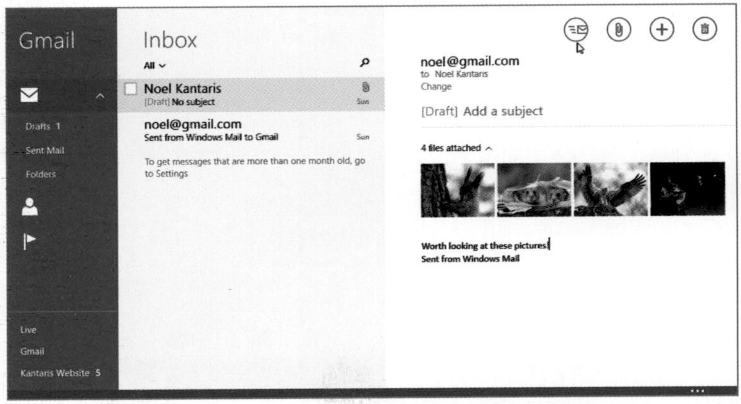

Fig. 5.10 An E-mail Message with Attached Photos.

All you have to do now is send the e-mail, perhaps to yourself, so you can see and check the result.

Note: Below the **Inbox** list, there is a link that you can use to see messages more that one month old. Try it!

Receiving Attachments

Fig. 5.11 below, shows the e-mail you'll receive with its attachments had you sent it to yourself.

Fig. 5.11 Received E-mail Message with Attached Photos.

The received message shows the (**.jpg**) pictures together with their name (if already named) and size and you are invited to **Download** them. Having done so, you can tap or click each picture to open the **Options** menu as shown in Fig. 5.12.

Fig. 5.12 Options to Open or Save Received Photos.

You can choose to **Open with** a particular program capable of editing the picture or to **Save** it, in which case a screen similar to that shown in Fig. 5.9 is displayed from where you can choose to go to another place to save the attachment other than your **Pictures** library by tapping or clicking the down-arrowhead against **Pictures** library.

Obviously, trying to save a document rather than a picture, **Mail** will attempt to save it to the **Document** library.

Deleting Messages

Some e-mail messages you receive will be worth keeping, but most will need deleting. From the **Read Message** window you just tap or click the **Delete** ⓘ button to do this. Whenever you delete a message it is actually moved to the **Deleted** folder.

Sending an E-mail to the Drafts Folder

If you decide that your e-mail is not complete yet and further changes are needed before sending it, use the **Delete** ⓘ button at the top right of the screen. This displays the screen in Fig. 5.13 on top of your e-mail.

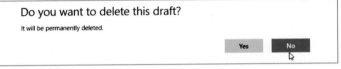

Do you want to delete this draft?

It will be permanently deleted.

| Yes | No |

Fig. 5.13 Saving E-mail as Draft.

To complete the process, tap or click the **No** button which saves your incomplete message to the **Drafts** folder, but also remains in the **Inbox** marked as **Draft**. This allows you to retrieve it later from either folder for further editing.

Summary of System Folders

The number and exact name of folders available in **Mail** depend on which account you are using. To see these, tap or click the **Folders** option on the **Folders** list. Most of these have been discussed already, but here is a summary of their function.

- The **Inbox** holds all incoming messages. These can be moved or copied into any other folder except the **Outbox** folder.

- The **Outbox** folder holds messages that have been prepared but not yet transmitted. As soon as the messages are sent they are automatically removed to the **Sent** folder.

- The **Sent** folder holds messages that have been trans-mitted. You can then decide whether to 'file' copies of these messages, or whether to delete them. Messages in the **Sent** folder can be moved or copied into any of the other folders except the **Outbox** folder.

- The **Deleted** or **Bin** folder holds messages that have been deleted and placed in there as a safety feature. Messages in the **Deleted** or **Bin** folder can be moved or copied into any of the other folders, except the **Outbox** folder.

- The **Drafts** folder is used to hold a message you started and tried to delete and selected the **No** option from the displayed banner. Messages in the **Drafts** folder cannot be moved or copied into any of the other folders. Simply tap or click such a message to open it, edit it, and then send it.

- The **Junk** folder (also referred to as **Spam** by some e-mail accounts) is designed to catch unsolicited messages.

To **Move** an e-mail from one folder to another, tap or click the small square in front of it to select it. This displays the appropriate button in a band at the bottom of the screen.

Printing Messages

Occasionally you might receive an important e-mail message that you would like to print and file for safe keeping. This is easy once you are shown how to do it.

First, display the e-mail you want to print on your computer's screen, then activate the **Charms** bar and tap or click **Devices** (see Fig. 2.16, page 20), which opens its window and displays the printers available to you, as shown in Fig. 5.14 on the next page. Your screen will most certainly look different, but it is assumed here that the printer you want to use is connected to your computer and switched on. It is also assumed that what you display on your screen is the actual e-mail message, not a screen in **Internet Explorer** associated with the e-mail.

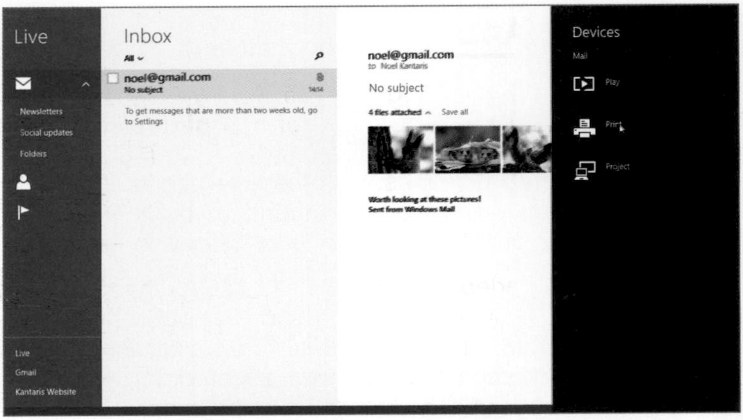

Fig. 5.14 The Message and Devices Options.

All you have to do to print the e-mail message is to tap or click the **Print** option and select your printer, to display a screen similar to that in Fig. 5.15. Tapping or clicking on the **Print** button starts the process.

Fig. 5.15 The Printer Options.

The People App

Windows **Mail** lets you create and keep a list of **People** (also called 'contacts') to store details such as the names, addresses, phone numbers and e-mail addresses of all those you communicate with most.

If you have upgraded to Windows 8.1, your 'contacts' would have automatically been transferred across, but if you have installed Windows 8.1 from Windows 7, then your **People** list will contain only the contacts you have added or imported into the program from mail accounts you add to Windows **Mail**. If you add **Live Mail** or **Gmail** into Windows **Mail**, then the 'contacts' list associated with these services will be transported across.

If all is well, selecting the **People** App on the **Start** screen, should change your screen to one similar to that in Fig. 5.16.

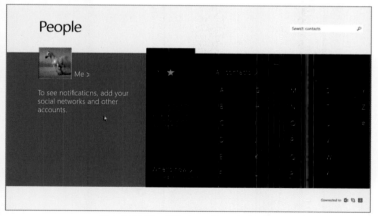

Fig. 5.16 The Windows People List.

In Fig. 5.16, a photo of you is expected, but in my case the white horse is preferable! Note that now you can jump to the beginning of each alphabetical section of your contacts' list, without having to scroll from A all the way to Z.

Note that in Fig. 5.16 shown on the previous page, you now have the ability to add to **Favourites** the details of people

who matter to you by tapping or clicking the **Favourites** button shown here enlarged.

This opens your contacts list for you to choose the people you want as your **Favourites**. As each is selected, you can add them to the list by tapping or clicking the ⌐Add⌐ button that becomes active at the bottom of the screen.

Fig. 5.17 An Added Contact to the Favourite List.

As you add more contacts to the **Favourite** list, its panel expands to accommodate them. To remove a contact from the list, tap or click on its icon, then tap or click the **Favourite**

button, as shown in Fig. 5.18, to deselect this contact from the list.

Fig. 5.18 Removing a Contact From the Favourite List.

You can add a new contact by first swiping upwards from the bottom of the screen or right-clicking to reveal the **Tools** bar at the bottom of the screen, then selecting the **Add** ⊕ button to display the screen shown in Fig. 5.19 below.

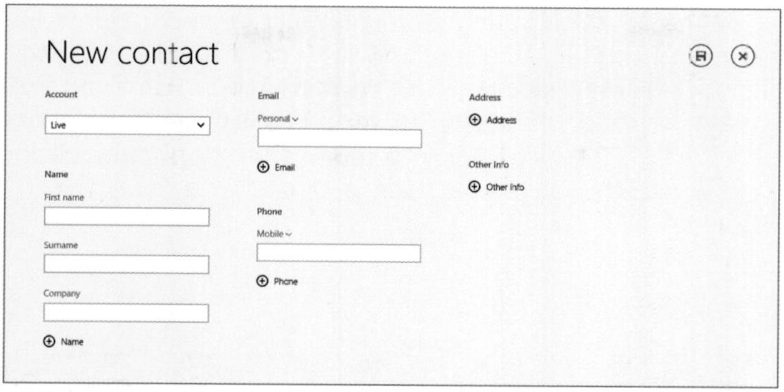

New contact   ⊞ ⊗

Account   Email   Address

Live   ∨   Personal ∨   ⊕ Address

                           ⊕ Email   Other info
Name   ⊕ Other info
First name   Phone

                           Mobile ∨
Surname
                           ⊕ Phone
Company

⊕ Name

Fig. 5.19 Adding a New Contact.

You can now enter the name, phone, and e-mail details for your new contact. Personal information can be entered now or later by editing the contact's entry. Once all is done, tap or click the **Save** ⓡ button.

To edit or delete a contact created within the **People**'s App,

tap it or click it to open it in its own screen, then swipe upwards or right-click to reveal the **Tools** bar at the bottom of the screen and select either the **Edit** 🖉 button or the **Delete** 🗑 button.

Fig. 5.20 Selecting a Mail Recipient.

Note: Contacts added from within the **People**'s App can be deleted. Imported contacts have to be deleted from the program of their origin and re-imported or simply ignored!

To send a new message from your **Contact**'s list, open their entry in the **People** list, as shown in Fig. 5.20 on the previous page, and tap or click the **Send email** 🔘 button to open a pre-addressed **New Message** window in **Mail**.

One rather nice touch here is that, if you have already entered an address for this person in their details, tapping or clicking the **Map address** 🔘 button (hidden in Fig. 5.20), displays a map showing the person's address, as shown below.

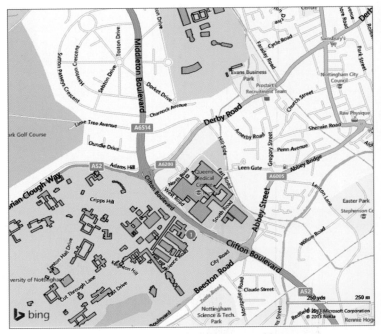

Fig. 5.21 A Contact's Address on a Map.

The screen above displays the University of Nottingham with the Department where my contact works identified with the blue circle. This map is shown in the **Maps** App, which will be discussed in detail in the next Chapter. You can even get directions to the address where your contact is to be found. For reasons of security, I have removed the name and exact address from the above screen.

The Calendar App

The Windows 8.1 **Start** screen also provides you with a **Calendar** tile which when you tap or click, opens the screen shown in Fig. 5.22.

November 2013 ⌄

Monday	Tuesday	Wednesday	Thursday	Friday	Saturday	Sunday
28	29	30	31	1	2	3
4	This is a recurring event. **Open one** **Open series** Lila's birthday ⌐		7	8	9	10
11	12	13	14	15	16	17
18	19	20	21	22	23	24
25	26	27	28	29	30	1

Fig. 5.22 The Opened Calendar.

Above, an entry was tapped or clicked to display the message **This is a recurring event** and underneath **Open one** or **Open Series**. As a recurring event, there is obviously a series of repeated events which you can choose to open so that you can edit the entry, as shown in Fig. 5.23.

← Noel's calendar
noel@live.com

Lila's birthday

When
05 November 2013 ⌄

Add a message

Start
0 ⌄ 00 ⌄

How long
All day ⌄

Location
St. Ives

Who
Invite people

Show more

Fig. 5.23 Editing a
Calendar Entry.

Similarly, you can make a new entry in your calendar, by tapping or clicking on a given day to display the screen below. Here, the **Show more** link in Fig. 5.23 has been activated, so more information is displayed, as shown in Fig. 5.24

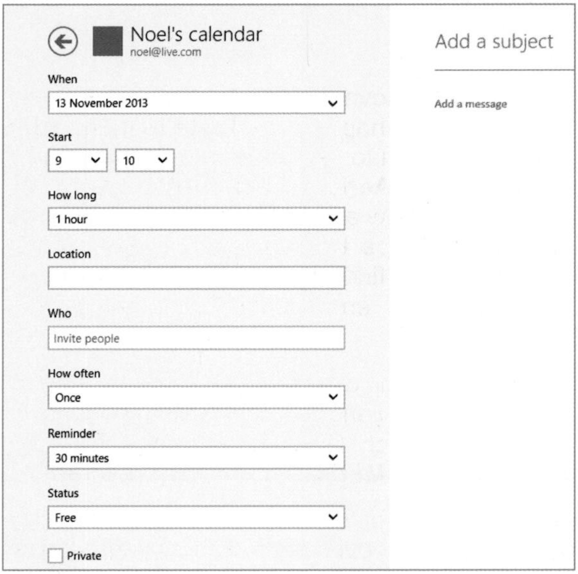

Fig. 5.24
Entering a
New Calendar
Entry.

This provides you with all the scheduling tools you will ever need. You can enter appointments, birthdays, or fix meetings with other people and invite them to the meeting. It also supports day, week and month views, as shown in Fig. 5.25.

Fig. 5.25 The Toolbar of the Main Calendar Screen.

These can be activated by tapping or clicking the **Show more commands**

button shown here enlarged (for its position, have a look at the bottom right corner of Fig. 5.22).

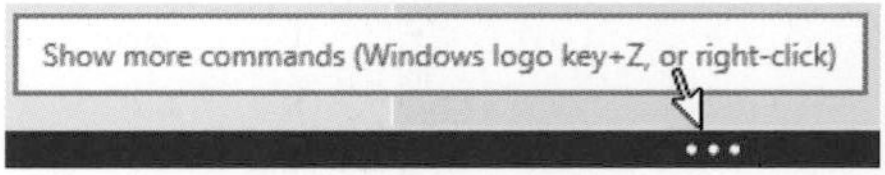

It is worth spending sometime exploring this excellent facility.

6

Bing Maps

Maps

I hope you love maps as much as I do, because this chapter is dedicate to them. **Bing Maps** help you to see a 2D view of the world in **Road** view, **Aerial** view, **Bird's eye** view, **Streetside** view and finally a **3D** view. You can use **Bing Maps** to plan your holiday, search for locations and addresses, find local services, get driving or walking directions, or just to enjoy looking at maps in their various views.

Bing Maps are available all over the world and its satellite imagery covers the entire planet, but at varying levels of resolution. You can approach **Bing Maps** either from the **Desktop** or by activating the **Maps** tile on the **Start** screen.

Bing Maps is an example of 'cloud computing' as you view maps in a Web browser and everything is downloaded from the Internet. The maps load quickly, especially if a reasonably fast Broadband connection is available, otherwise a little patience might be needed!

The Desktop Bing Maps Environment

Once your browser is open you can open **Bing Maps** in one of two ways. You can type **www.bing.com/maps** into the **Address** bar of your browser and press the **Enter** key, or you can tap or click the **Maps** link in the **Bing Navigation** bar of any **Bing** page, as shown in Fig. 6.1 below.

| WEB | IMAGES | VIDEOS | MAPS | NEWS | SEARCH HISTORY | MORE | | MSN | | OUTLOOK.COM |

Get directions/traffic

Fig. 6.1 The Bing Navigation Bar.

With either of these methods the opening screen should look like that in Fig. 6.2 below.

Fig. 6.2 The Opening Screen for the UK Bing Maps.

You can now type in a location, such as **bath, somerset, uk**, to get a screen similar to that in Fig. 6.3 below.

Fig. 6.3 A Search Screen for the UK Bing Maps Using a Location.

Tapping or clicking the **Zoom** link within the black oblong above, allows you to zoom in or out to see more or less detail of the area.

Map Views

Depending on your location, there are different map views available in **Bing Maps**. These are controlled by the links at the top the map area, as shown in Fig. 6.2 on the previous page. When the mouse pointer hovers over the down-arrowheads of these two links, it displays other links, as shown in Fig. 6.4.

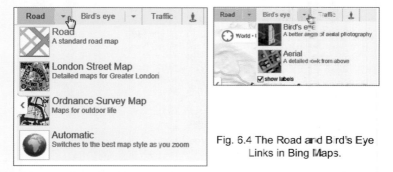

Fig. 6.4 The Road and Bird's Eye
Links in Bing Maps.

You tap or click these links to change between the available views. In general, these links have the following effect:

Road – Displays a traditional style of map with a depiction of roads, borders, rivers, parks and lakes, etc.

Bird's eye – Displays aerial imagery of the same area. To show road and street names, select **Labels** on its drop-down options. The displayed images are not current and their quality depends on the locality.

Traffic – Displays visual traffic data for motorways and major trunk roads.

Ordnance Survey – This link on the drop-down **Roads** options in Fig. 6.4, displays **Ordnance Survey Maps** of the area. You'll need to zoom in or use a magnifying glass to see details!

Perhaps it might be worthwhile spending some time here to see the effect of all these links – far too many to give precise description of their effect. Experimenting in this case is by far the best way of finding out for yourself.

Searching for a Location

If you want to find details of a particular location you just search for it. This is a **bing** program after all! You can search for an address, city, town, airport, county, country or continent by typing details in the **Search** box and tapping or clicking the **Search** button, as shown below.

Fig. 6.5 Entering a Search Address.

The result of this search is shown in Fig. 6.6 below. **Bing** jumped to a map of the Cornish town, placed a 'marker' on it and showed the search result in text in the left pane of the display.

Fig. 6.6 The Result of a Search for a Town in Ordnance Survey Map View.

For specific addresses, entering them in the form of **Address, town, post code** usually gives the best results. You can also search for geographic features such as parks, mountains, lakes, etc., in the same way.

In Fig. 6.6, the left pane displays a selection of **Nearby** options based on the current map location. Tapping or clicking the **eat+drink** link displays a whole list of such places with their addresses and numerical markers showing their location on the map, as shown in Fig. 6.7 on the next page.

Note that the map below is displayed in Ordinance Survey view.

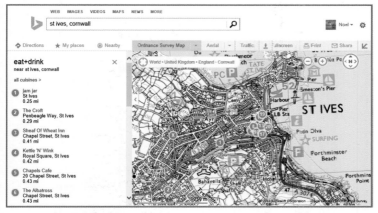

Fig. 6.7 The Result of a Search in Ordnance Survey View.

To exit the **eat+drink** view, tap or click the **x** icon that appears just outside the top left corner of the map. To look up other 'nearby' options tap or click the **Search X** button again.

   Do not confuse the 'blue' ⊚ Nearby button in Fig. 6.7 above with the 'orange' NEARBY in Fig. 6.6. The former means nearby the town you are looking at, while the latter means activities within the town you are displaying. Rather unfortunate choice of name for describing such different activities!

Searching for Services

No matter where you are in the country, you can use **Bing Maps** to find the nearest business, educational or amusement service. Enter the appropriate words followed by the words **in** or **near**, and the town, city or other location in the **Search** box. For example, typing *galleries in st ives cornwall* in the **Search** box and selecting **Bird s eye** view, displays the screen in Fig. 6.8, shown on the next page, when you tap or click the **Search** button.

Bing shows the results of the search in the left panel and a map of the area in the right panel, with markers linked to the results, as shown in Fig. 6.8 below.

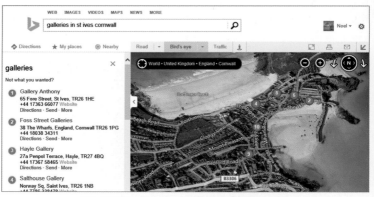

Fig. 6.8 The Result of a Search for Galleries.

However, the Tate gallery in St. Ives is not amongst those listed above – it only happens to be the most famous one! Even adding the word 'art' in front the search criteria doesn't find the Tate, although it does find others. To find it, you must almost ask for it by name, as shown in Fig. 6.9.

Fig. 6.9 The Info Window.

Navigating the Map Area

With **Bing Maps** you can change what shows in the map viewing area in two dimensions. You can pan the map (move it across the screen at the same scale), and you can zoom it in (to see a smaller area in more detail) or out (to see a larger area with less detail). You can navigate around a map using either your finger, the mouse or the supplied **Navigation** controls shown at the top-right corner in Fig. 6.8 above.

Using your finger, you can move around a map by simply touching it and moving in the direction you want to go. To zoom out you just place two fingers on the map and bring them together in a pinch movement and to zoom in you spread your fingers outwards (see Appendix A).

Using the mouse can also execute all the necessary operations easily and quickly. For example, to pan the map, just hold the left mouse button down to change the mouse pointer to a hand ᶜᵐ⁾ which you use to drag the map around the screen. To zoom in, just roll the mouse wheel away from you, and towards you to zoom out. The zoom will centre on the pointer location on the map.

With these actions (fingers or mouse) you can almost instantly zoom out to view the whole Earth, as shown in Fig. 6.10 in 'Bird's eye' view, then move the pointer to a new location and zoom in again to the scale you need. You can also centre and zoom in on a location, by double-tapping or double-clicking it on the map.

Fig. 6.10 An Aerial View of the Whole Earth.

To pan the map, you use a finger or point with your mouse and left-click, then drag the map to move it to the direction you want to go.

You can use the two **Navigation** controls to zoom in ⊕ on the centre of the map, and ⊖ to zoom out.

If you prefer using the keyboard, you can zoom in and out with the + and − keys. You can pan left ⇐, right ⇒, up ⇑, and down ⇓ with the arrow keys. The choice is yours!

Getting Directions

There are several ways in **Bing Maps** to get directions from one location to another. You can type a **from-to** statement into the search field, such as *from st ives cornwall to oxford*, and tap or click the **Search** button; you can tap or click the **Directions** link, enter a starting and ending location and tap or click the **Go** button or get directions from an info window (see Fig. 6.6, page 90).

The first method actually completes the operation as if you had used the second method, as shown in Fig. 6.11 below.

Fig. 6.11 Getting Driving Directions.

The program defaults to giving driving directions and the

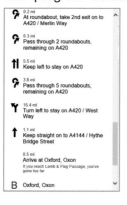

recommended route appears on the map as a blue line with green and red markers at either end, as shown in Fig. 6.11 above. **Bing Maps** give a total distance, as shown on the left panel of Fig. 6.11 and suggests suitable routes in its detailed numbered directions (you might have to scroll down to see these), part of which is shown in Fig. 6.12.

Fig. 6.12 The Suggested Route.

If you tap or click on a route section in the left panel, an enlarged map opens, as shown in Fig. 6.13.

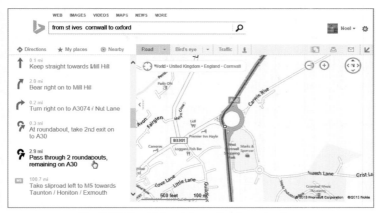

Fig. 6.13 Street View Information for a Section.

The **Bird's eye** view of the above map is worth seeing, as displayed below in Fig. 6.14.

Fig. 6.14 Bird's Eye View for a Section of the Map.

When you study the proposed route on the map you may find you want to alter it. That's no problem with **Bing Maps**. You can just drag a point on the blue directions line to any location on the map. As an example, I decided to take the scenic route to Oxford, as shown in Fig. 6.15, but doing so has increased the journey time by 1 hour from the originally suggested route, even though it is half a mile less!

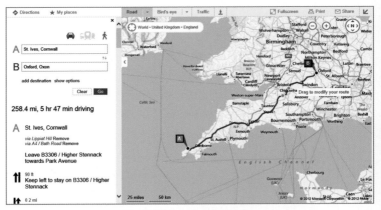

Fig. 6.15 The Scenic Route.

Public Transport

Depending on where you are, the **Public Transport** feature of **Bing Maps** may let you map your trip using train, bus and coach transport. If transit information is available when you search for directions between start and end locations in **Bing Maps**, the **Public Transport** option 🚇 will appear under the **Directions** option, as shown in Fig. 6.16 on the next page.

The times of departure of the various methods of public transport are given in the left panel. Again you'll have to scroll down to see these. To plan your trip in the future, click the down-arrowheads and select a new date and time.

This feature could be very useful, but until much better coverage is available in the UK you would be best using it with care.

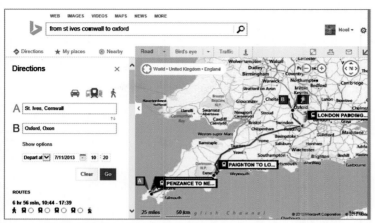

Fig. 6.16 A Set of Public Transport Directions in Road View.

Printing Bing Maps

You can print both **Road** view maps and **Bird's eye** view maps with their direction information in **Bing Maps**. With the map area you want to print on the screen, tap or click the **Print** 🖶 icon at the top right of the map area to display an additional screen in which you can choose to print the **Map and text**, **Map only** or **Text only**. With the first option, under the main map you also get detailed maps of the start and end destinations of your choice, as shown in Fig. 6.17 below.

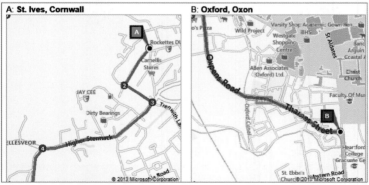

Fig. 6.17 Direction Maps of Start and End Destinations.

Streetside View

If you tap or click the **Streetside** view ![icon] icon at the top of the map area, the cursor changes to a blue 'Peg Man' as shown here, with the map itself displaying blue areas within which a **Streetside** view is available (Fig. 6.18).

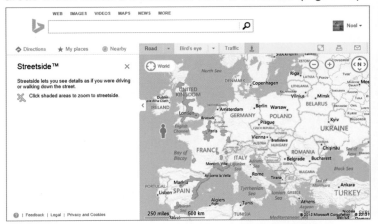

Fig. 6.18 Available Streetside View Area Coverage.

The blue blotches on the above map of Europe, show the available areas of **Streetside** views. The moment you move the 'Peg Man' to <u>anyone</u> of these, the screen changes to that of Fig. 6.19.

Fig. 6.19 The Microsoft Silverlight Installation.

As you can see from the note at the top right of the screen, you'll need to download Microsoft's **Silverlight** App, if you don't have it already. Just follow the on-screen instructions.

Tapping or clicking the **Start the map app**, the **Silverlight** App is installed within half a minute and the screen changes to one similar, but not necessarily the same as in Fig. 6.20.

Fig. 6.20 A Streetside View Display.

To use the **Streetside** view effectively, it is best to exit the above view, then use **bing** to search for a known address. Surprisingly, neither Oxford nor Cambridge are available in this view, but Bristol is.

So, let us search for the **Streetside** view of 'Royal York Crescent, Clifton, Bristol'. To achieve this, do the following:

• Start **Maps** in **Internet Explorer**.

• Type the search criteria given above in **bing** and tap or click the search button.

• When the road map of the area is displayed on your screen, press the **Search** ⌕ button.

• When **bing** finds the location, press the **Streetside** View ⬇ icon to change the pointer to the blue 'Peg Man'.

Placing this on the desired location displays the screen shown in Fig. 6.21 on the next page.

Fig. 6.21 A Streetside View of the Royal York Crescent in Clifton.

There are several things to remember when you display a location in **Streetside** view. These are:

- To move to a required position on a street, drag the street to the focus in the small preview window at the top-right corner of the display, not the other way round.

- To change the viewing direction use the curved arrows on the navigation control.

- To zoom in or out, tap or click the ⊕ or ⊖ buttons.

- As you move the mouse pointer within **Streetside** view, you'll notice that the 'Peg Man' changes its stance; upright when you are following a road or pointing right or left. Tapping or clicking the latter, moves what you see in the direction pointed by the 'Peg Man'.

- Sometimes the pointer changes to a magnifying glass with either a **+** or a **-** sign on it. Tapping or clicking such a pointer zooms you in or out.

Again, the only way of getting familiar with **Streetside** view is by trying to use it and experimenting with the pointer.

Once you have found the area you want to explore with **Streetside** view, tap or click the **Enter full screen mode** button to view a larger **Streetside** view area. To return **Streetside** view to its previous size, tap or click the **Exit full screen mode** button.

To exit **Streetside** view, tap of click the ← Exit button which returns you to **Road** view.

Sharing Maps

If you tap or click the link pointed to in Fig. 6.22 at the top of the **bing Maps** main window (you might have to increase the width of the window to see it), you can e-mail the current map or directions to a friend or colleague.

Fig. 6.22 The Share Link.

This **Share** button when clicked displays the small window shown in Fig. 6.23.

Fig. 6.23 The Link Window.

From here you can either have a copy of the URL inserted in the body of an e-mail message when you click the **send** button, or copy and paste the HTML code to embed the current map into a Web page. You can then either e-mail directly to a friend, or make the information available in **Facebook** or **Twitter**.

Traffic View

Bing Maps has an exciting feature, that provides traffic data for the motorways and major A roads in England, Scotland, and parts of Europe.

In Fig. 6.24 below, I show the **Road** map view of a specific area, Clifton in Bristol, so that you can compare this map with the **Traffic** version of the same area.

Whatever map view you are in, if you tap or click the **Traffic** link, the parts of motorways and trunk roads that are subject to traffic hold ups will be overlayed with colour, as shown in Fig. 6.25, also shown below.

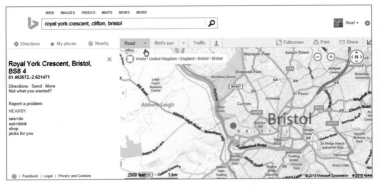

Fig. 6.24 Road View Around Clifton.

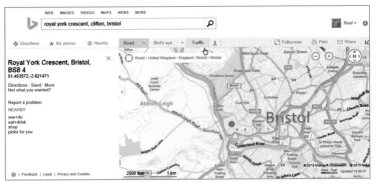

Fig. 6.25 Traffic View Around Clifton.

If your route shows red, it's stop-and-go for you, while green means it is probably clear, as shown here. This is a very good feature when you are about to  start your journey, but not so good if you are driving at the time, unless you have a tablet device with you! The map was updated only 10 min ago from writing.

When you are finished, click the **Traffic** link again to deselect it and turn off the feature.

The Maps App

If you tap or click the **Maps** App tile on the Windows 8.1 **Start** screen, what displays first is a map of your location (if you have given your permission to be located). Swiping upwards from the bottom of the screen or right-clicking, displays the **bing Toolbar** at the bottom of the screen, as shown in Fig. 6.26.

Fig. 6.26 The Bing Toolbar.

From here, you can **Add a pin** to the map, choose a **Map style**, display **My location**, obtain **Directions** and **Find** places or services.

If you tap or click on **Map style**, you'll see that the choice is confined to either **Road view**, **Aerial view** or **Show traffic**, while the **Directions** tool opens a window on the top-right of the map screen as shown here in Fig. 6.27. Note that the program remembers the destinations you used when using **bing** from the **Desktop**. The only difference is that the starting point of your journey is assumed to be from your current location, although you can easily change this.

Fig. 6.27 The Directions Window.

A similar window is displayed if you tap or click **Find** on the toolbar, which also includes a list of suggested places taken from previous use of **bing**. If you type, say King's College Cambridge, you are told to refine your search. However, if you first search for **University Cambridge**, then tap or click the **Find** tool once more, but now type **King's College**, you are taken to the correct place.

In Fig. 6.28, King's College is displayed on **Aerial View**, but zoomed in so that its features are shown very clearly. Try it for yourself.

Fig. 6.28 Aerial View of King's College Cambridge.

To change the view to **Traffic**, you must first zoom out before the App can display what you want. You cannot print anything from within this App, but you can go to the **Desktop** version of **bing**'s **Map** option and get to the same display as the above before printing. Searching for King's College Cambridge on **bing**'s **Desktop** version, finds the location instantly!

As usual, the only way to find out how this App works is to try it. Have fun!

7

Photos, Videos & Music

In Windows 8.1, just as in its predecessor, you can use either the **File Explorer** on the **Desktop** to navigate to the **Libraries** which point to the **Pictures**, **Videos** and **Music** folders or use the tiles provided on the **Start** screen which are used by mobile users (meaning mainly tablet users).

The Desktop Pictures Library

Window 8.1 in its **Desktop** mode provides a library for your photos, called the **Pictures** library. It is the default location for saving pictures and importing them from your digital camera.

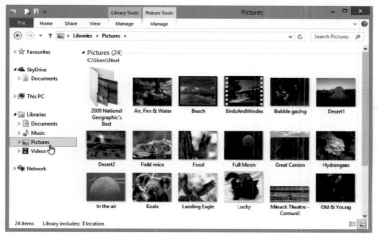

Fig. 7.1 Digital Photographs in the Pictures Folder.

I put most images I like in this folder, but keep my personal photos in sub-folders in another location on my hard drive.

The Picture Tools

In Fig. 7.1, the **Ribbon** is minimised. Expanding the **Ribbon** reveals tools that are mostly greyed out until a picture is selected. When that is done, then you can **Delete** the selected picture, **Rename** it, **Move** it, **Copy** it, etc.

Fig. 7.2 shows the tools available to you on the **Ribbon** when a picture is selected and the **Picture Tools** button is tapped or clicked. You can now **Rotate** the selected picture to the left or right, **Set** it as background, or start a **Slide show**.

Fig. 7.2 Picture Tools.

Other **Ribbon** options allow you to **Share** selected pictures with friends and family, as was discussed earlier. It might be worth spending some time here, going through the various **Toolbar** options, to discover for yourself what is available.

The Windows Photo Viewer

To see a larger view of a picture, touch and hold or right-click it to open a contextual menu, then choose the **Open with** option to display a further menu similar to that in Fig. 7.3.

Fig. 7.3 Program Options.

Selecting the **Windows Photo Viewer**, displays the photo as shown in Fig. 7.4 on the next page. The Toolbar at the top offers **File** options, **Print**, **E-mail**, or **Burn** the selected photo to a data disc or **Open** a photo for viewing or possibly editing.

Fig. 7.4 The Windows Photo Viewer.

You can use the controls at the bottom of the **Viewer** to navigate through the current folder, view the pictures in your folder as a slide show, zoom in or out, rotate the image, and delete it from your hard disc.

Printing Photos

Selecting a picture in the **Viewer** and clicking the **Print** option in the **Share** tab, displays the window shown below

Fig. 7.5 The Print Pictures Window.

From here you can select the **Printer** to be used, **Paper size**, **Quality** of print, **Paper Type** and a variety of layouts for your pictures. All you have to do then is click the **Print** button.

The Photos App

Clicking the **Photos** tile on the **Start** screen, displays the screen shown in Fig. 7.6 below. Do note, however, that the picture on the **Photos** App tile shown to the left, changes because the photos in the **Pictures** library are shown as a live slide show, therefore what is shown here is bound to be different for you.

Fig. 7.6 Location of Photos for the Mobile User.

Tapping or clicking the down-arrowhead against **Pictures library**, opens a menu of all possible locations for photos, namely **Pictures library** and **SkyDrive**. Tapping or clicking the button at the top right corner of the screen changes the display from **Details view** (the current display) to **Thumbnails view**.

Selecting a picture and swiping the screen upwards from the bottom edge, reveals a set of tools, as shown enlarged in Fig. 7.7 on the next page.

Fig. 7.7 The Set of Picture Tools.

You can use these tools to **Delete**, **Copy**, **Cut**, **Rename** or **Open with** a selection of one or more pictures. You can also create a **New folder** to insert into it a selection of pictures, **Import** picture from a camera or start a **Slideshow**.

Next, tapping or clicking the photo in the **Pictures library**, displays a new enlarged screen, as shown in Fig. 7.8.

Fig. 7.8 The Enlarged Picture and its Toolbar.

To reveal the tool options shown at the bottom of the above screen, either swipe upwards from the bottom of the screen or right-click. The options here are specific to the displayed picture and mainly allow you to **Delete**, **Rotate**, **Crop** or **Edit** it. There are, of course, additional tools for opening the picture with a particular program, start a **Slideshow**, etc.

To exit from the **Photos** App, drag the opened picture from the very top of the screen towards the bottom with your finger or use the mouse by placing its pointer at the top of the screen, then clicking the left mouse button to change the pointer from an open hand to a closed one and dragging the picture all the way to the bottom edge of the screen.

Getting Photos from a Device

Windows 8.1 makes the process of importing pictures from your digital camera or phone to your computer extremely simple.

Once you have taken some photos, connect the camera or phone to your computer with the appropriate USB cable, switch the device on and tap or click the **Portable Device** option on the displayed **Choose a device to import from** sub-screen that pops up. Next, tap or click the **Import** button on the toolbar at the bottom of the **Pictures library** screen pointed to in Fig. 7.9 to start the import process, shown in Fig. 7.10 below.

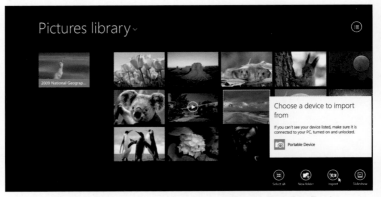

Fig. 7.9 The Process of Importing Pictures from a Portable Device.

Fig. 7.10 The Creation of a Special Folder to Import Pictures.

By default, a new folder appears in the **Pictures library** and given a name made up from the date the pictures were imported, like **2013-11-10** in this case, as displayed in Fig. 7.10.

You can also see this by using the **File Explorer** on the **Desktop** to look at the content of the **Pictures** library, as shown in Fig. 7.11.

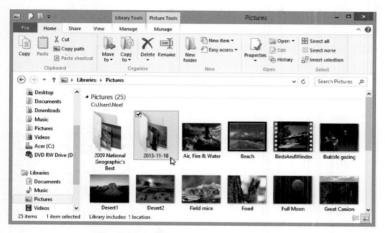

Fig. 7.11 A Collage of Imported Pictures.

When the process of importing your photos has finished a display for your device appears on the screen, as shown here in Fig. 7.12 for my phone, so that you can disconnect it from the computer.

Fig. 7.12.

Each photo in the folder is given a number which depends on your device. If you are happy with this, fine. If not you can spend a while renaming the folder and each picture.

If you are like me and you don't import your photos into your computer often enough, then this is the time to use the desktop **File Explorer** to create new folders with appropriate names and sort your photos now rather than later, as it is very easy to forget where each photo was taken! Do as I say, not as I do!

Scanning Photos

To import the images from paper photographs or slides into your computer you have to use a scanner. These are fairly cheap these days, in fact many printers include the ability to scan as well. To handle slides effectively though you need a special slide and negative scanner, but be warned these are not cheap!

Using the Windows Scan Facility

There are many ways to control a scanner using third party software but Windows 8.1 comes with its own program called **Windows Scan**, but you can only access it from the **Control Panel**.

With your scanner properly installed and turned on, you can open this program by tapping or clicking the **Desktop** tile on the **Start** screen, then opening the **Charms** bar shown in Fig. 7.13 and tapping or clicking the **Settings** charm. This opens the screen in Fig. 7.14 from which you can open the **Control Panel** shown in Fig. 7.15. In the **Control Panel**, tap or click the **Devices and Printers** entry pointed to in Fig. 7.15 below, to open a screen similar to that shown in Fig. 7.16 on the next page.

Fig. 7.13.

Fig. 7.14 The Settings Screen.

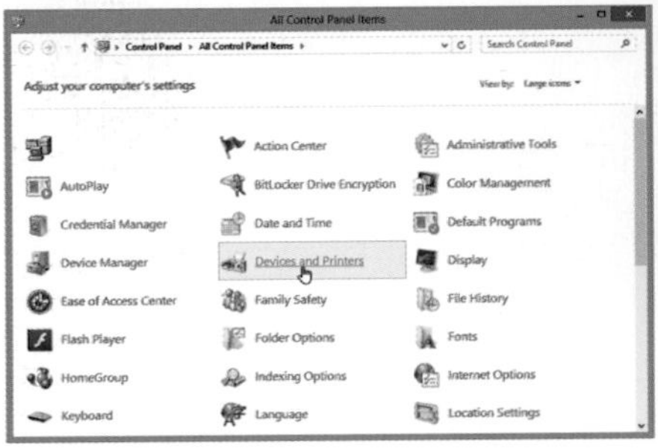

Fig. 7.15 The Control Panel Items.

Fig. 7.16 The Devices and Printers Screen.

Touch and hold or right-click the default printer (which happens to be an all-in-one type) to open a menu of options as shown in Fig. 7.17 below.

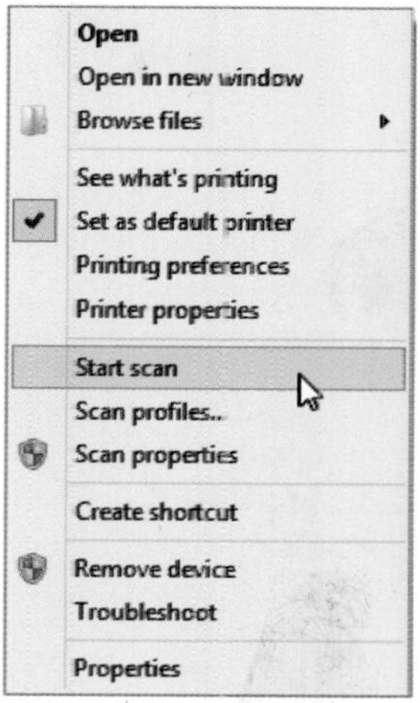

Open
Open in new window
Browse files   ▶

See what's printing
✔ Set as default printer
Printing preferences
Printer properties

Start scan
Scan profiles...
Scan properties

Create shortcut

Remove device
Troubleshoot

Properties

Fig. 7.17 The Right-click Menu.

From this menu of options you can set the **Scan Profiles** and **Scan Properties** and finally use the **Start scan** option to open the screen shown in Fig. 7.18.

It is assumed that you have placed your photo on the scanner before using the **Preview** option so that you can limit the actual scan to the correct size by dragging the handles of the cropping tool.

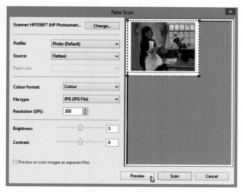

Fig. 7.18 The Preview of the Scanned Photo.

Having done so, you can use the **Scan** button to start the actual scan, after which the screen shown in Fig. 7.19 on the next page is displayed.

On this screen you can choose to **Review** or **Import** the scanned photo before pressing the **Next** button. Accepting the default setting and pressing the **Next** button, displays the screen shown

Fig. 7.19 The Import Pictures and Videos Screen.

in Fig. 7.20 where you can enter a name, add a tag, etc., before finally importing it into its own folder available to the **Pictures** library.

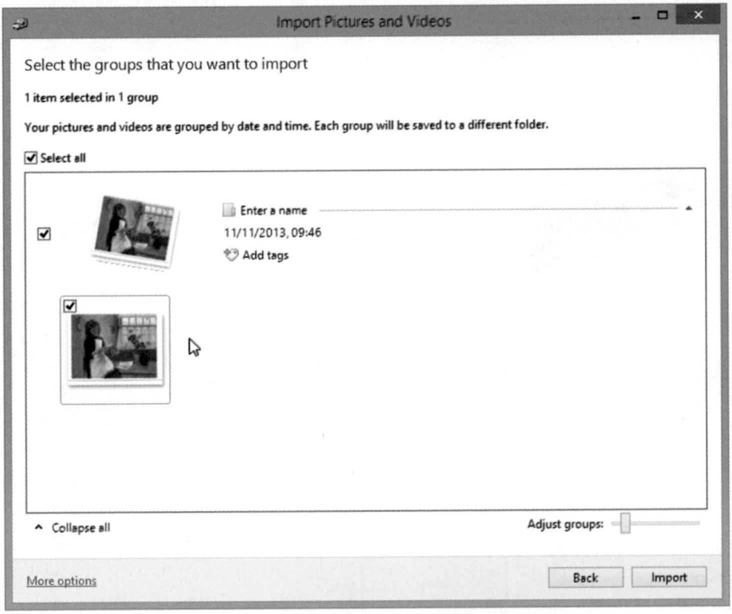

Fig. 7.20 The Import Pictures and Videos Screen.

The **Windows Scan** facility is not particularly intuitive, but it is easy enough to work with once you find out how to do it. The folder created and available to the **Pictures** library is similar to that created when you import pictures from a camera.

The Desktop Videos Library

In its **Desktop** mode, Windows 8.1 provides a library for your videos, called the **Videos** library. It is the default location for saving videos you might have received as attachments to e-mail messages, or imported from your video recorder.

Fig. 7.21 The Videos Folder.

The Video Tools

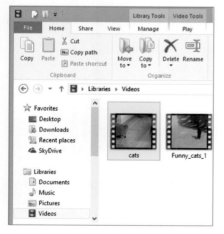

In Fig. 7.21 above, the **Ribbon** tools are mostly greyed out until a video is selected as shown in Fig. 7.22. When that is done, then you can **Delete** the selected video, **Rename** it, **Move** it, **Copy** it, etc., while other **Ribbon** options allow you to **Share** selected videos.

Fig. 7.22 Video Tools.

The Windows Video App

To start a video playing, double-tap or double-click it to open it in the **Windows Video** App, as shown in Fig. 7.23 below.

Fig. 7.23 The Windows Video App.

If you now revert to the **Start** screen of Windows 8.1, you'll see that the **Video** tile displays the name of the last video you played. In your case this is bound to be different. If you now tap or click the **Video** tile, a screen similar to the one in Fig. 7.24 is displayed.

Fig. 7.24 Part of the Contents of the Video App.

On the left of the screen in Fig. 7.24 shown on the previous page, all the videos available to your **Videos** library are displayed (not shown in the screen dump on Fig. 7.24), while to the right of the screen thumbnails of videos, films or TV shows are displayed. When you tap or click one of these, a small window opens giving details of each item and giving you the opportunity to either purchase or rent a DVD or watch a trailer.

The Desktop Music Library

In its **Desktop** mode, Windows 8.1 provides a library for your music, called the **Music** library. It is the default location for saving music you might have downloaded, or imported from a CD.

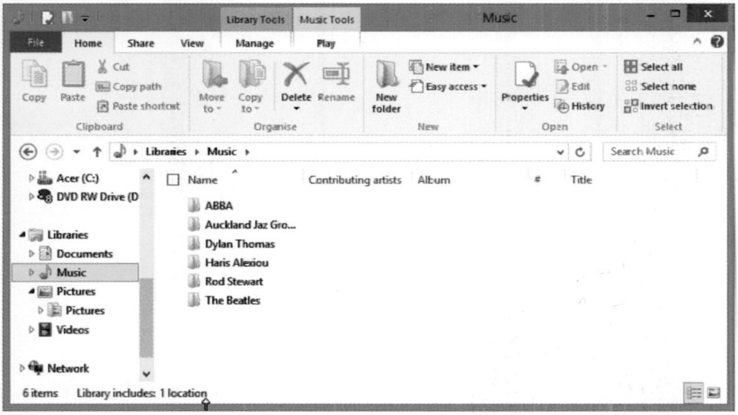

Fig. 7.25 The Music Folder.

The Music Tools

In Fig. 7.25 above, the **Ribbon** tools are mostly greyed out, just as they are for the other **Library** folders until a music folder or track is selected. When that is done, then you can **Delete** the selected music folder or track, **Rename** it, **Move** it, **Copy** it, etc., while other **Ribbon** options allow you to **Share** selected music with your **HomeGroup**.

The Windows Music App

To start a music track playing, double-tap or double-click it to open it in the **Windows Music** App, as shown in Fig. 7.26.

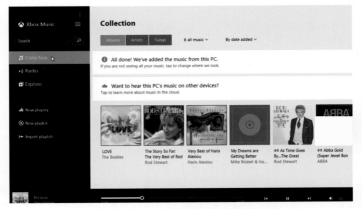

Fig. 7.26 The Windows Music App.

This is the identical screen you'll get if you revert to the **Start** screen of Windows 8.1 and tap or click the **Music** tile shown here. On the left of the screen there are several options. Selecting **Radio** opens the screen below.

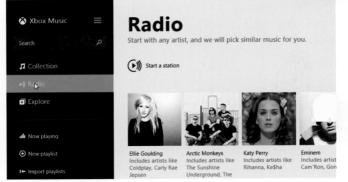

Fig. 7.27 The Radio Option of Xbox.

The **xbox** music player is intuitive, so do explore it by yourself.

8

Media Player & Media Center

Both **Media Player** and **Media Center** have been designed to handle all your digital media content, such as digital music, videos, photos, recorded TV shows and streamed Internet media.

Media files, as expected, are saved by default to the **Music** and **Video** libraries automatically by the media programs described here. The **Media Player** is available to both Windows 8.1 and Windows 8.1 Pro, but not to Windows RT.

However, Microsoft has decided to remove DVD playback from both Windows 8 and 8.1, as the Operating System was primarily designed for ultrabooks, tablets and hybrid PCs that lack optical drives. So now **Windows Media Player** can only play your music and your videos and display your pictures.

Note: If you want to play DVDs on your computer's optical drive, you must download and install **Media Center** which is only available to you if you upgrade from Windows 8.1 to Windows 8.1 Pro Pack, then apply to Microsoft for a product 'key' to allow you to download and install **Media Center**.

The Desktop Windows Media Player

 The **Desktop** Windows **Media Player** is the main media 'workhorse' in Windows 8.1. It has been around for a few years now. It provides a good-looking, intuitive and easy-to-use desktop interface for you to play the digital media files stored on your computer, or on CDs, or other external storage devices.

You can organise your digital media collection, rip music from your CDs to the computer and burn CDs of your favourite music, so you can play them on your home system or in your car.

It also lets you sync (synchronise) digital media files to a large range of portable media devices (but not Apple iPods and iPads unfortunately), and encourages you to shop for digital media content online. In other words, with **Media Player** you can play your audio and video material, view it, organise it, or sync it, but not your DVDs.

Searching for the Media Player

By default, the **Windows Media Player** is not pinned on the **Taskbar**, where it would be convenient to have it. So, the first thing to do is find it using the **Search** charm, as shown in the composite screen dump in Fig. 8.1 below.

First, swipe from the right edge of the screen towards the left or place the mouse pointer at the top-right corner of the screen, to reveal the **Charms** bar, then tap or click the **Search** charm. This opens a separate screen, shown at the top of Fig. 8.1, where you can type your search criteria.

As you type, a number of Apps appear on the screen which reduce in number as you continue typing. Eventually the App you are looking for is displayed on the screen.

To pin this App on the **Taskbar**, touch and hold or right-click it to display the options, as shown here, and tap or click the **Pin to Taskbar** option to complete the operation.

Fig. 8.1 Searching for Media Player.

Starting Media Player

By default, tapping or clicking the **Windows Media Player** 🔘 button on the **Taskbar** will open the program, unless you already have installed **Media Center** in which case the latter displays.

Media Player displays many views of your media, but if you have a CD in your optical drive it might, when started, look something similar to that in Fig. 8.2 below.

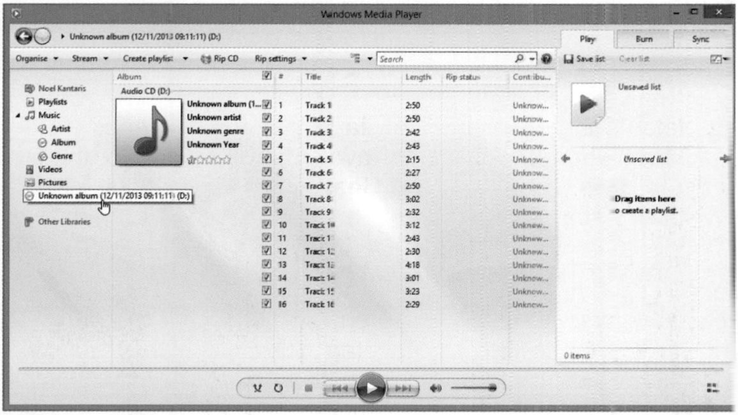

Fig. 8.2 A Player View of a Music CD.

If the **Media Player** does not recognise the CD automatically it will show as an **Unknown album**, as in the above case.

It is usually easy to correct this by touching and holding or right-clicking the default album artwork graphic shown here and selecting the **Find album info** option. In this case the artist's name and the album title are known and are automatically inserted in the **Search** box (you might have to type this information, if it isn't picked up automatically), then tap or click the **Search** button and hopefully select the correct album from the list offered as shown in Fig. 8.3 on the next page.

Fig. 8.3 Finding Album Information for a CD.

Finally, after you have made the correct selection, tap or click the **Next** button, check that the track information is correct and select **Finish** to accept the displayed information, as shown in Fig. 8.4 below.

Fig. 8.4 Displaying Album Information for a CD.

This might not be your type of music, but it was specially chosen to illustrates the point. However, this should be done after ripping the tracks to your library (see next section) so the information can be retained, as it cannot be copied to the CD!

Ripping from Audio CDs

The tracks and songs on an inserted CD will not show in your **Library** unless you 'rip' them from the CD. This is not as destructive as it sounds. It simply means copying tracks from the CD to the library on your computer's hard disc, so that you can listen to them whenever you want to.

By default, Windows **Media Player** rips to **.wma** format with CD quality encoding. This is good enough for me, but if you want to change these settings click **Rip settings** on the **Button** bar and choose **More options**.

The tracks ready to be ripped from the inserted audio CD (see Fig. 8.2, page 121) display in the **Details** pane (in conjunction with the album art and all the album tracks named in Fig. 8.4 on the previous page), ready to be copied to your library.

If there are any tracks that you don't want to rip, clear the check box next to them (Fig. 8.2). When you are ready, click the **Rip CD** button on the **Button** bar, shown here, to start the process. You will be warned about licence requirements, etc., after which ripping begins.

By default the selected tracks are copied to the **Music** library on your PC with folders added and labelled with the name of the artist or group.

While the ripping operation is in progress you can see exactly what is going on by looking at the **Rip status** column. You can listen to the CD while you are ripping it, so you needn't get too bored. By the time you listen to one track, the whole process would have completed.

To cancel ripping at any time, just tap or click the **Stop rip** button. Once you have ripped one CD you will find it very easy to rip your whole collection.

Player View Modes

Media Player lets you toggle between two main view modes. The **Player Library** shown in Fig. 8.5 below, which gives you control of all the **Player**'s features, and a **Now Playing** mode, shown in Fig. 8.6, which gives a simplified view ideal for playback.

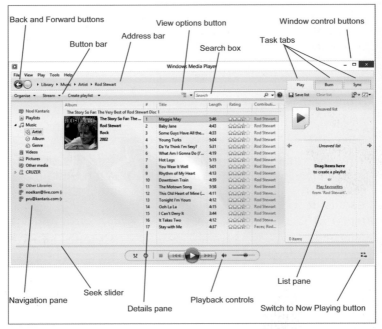

Fig. 8.5 Parts of the Player Library Window.

To move between these modes click the **Switch to Now Playing** button, or from the **Media Player**, the **Switch to Library** button in the upper-right corner pointed to in Fig. 8.6.

Fig. 8.6 Now Playing Mode.

When you tap or click an item, such as **Music** in the **Navigation** pane it lists your media content in the **Details** pane. Tapping or clicking on **Artist** will list your music files by artist and double-tapping or double-clicking on a CD icon, lists the tracks on that CD. Double-tapping or double-clicking on a track name will start it playing in the **Media Player**.

There are three different viewing options in the **Details** pane, chosen from a drop-down menu by tapping or clicking the arrow next to the **View options** button, shown here in Fig. 8.7, or by just tapping or clicking the button itself repeatedly until you get the view you want.

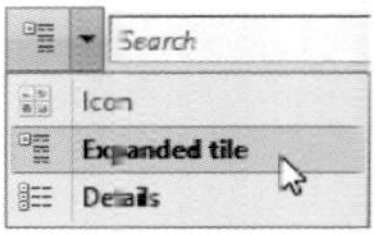

Fig. 8.7 The View Options.

Searching a Library

When you want to find a specific artist, album title or song name, you can simply type a search string in the **Search** box as shown in Fig. 8.8. For example, typing **help** immediately presents results of the search (top-half of Fig 8.8) and tapping or clicking on it, displays another screen with the actual details (bottom-half of Fig. 8.8) naming the **Beatles** album and the track number in this example.

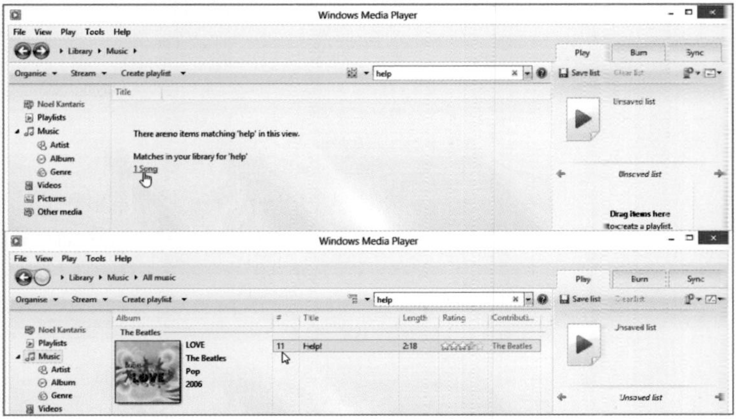

Fig. 8.8 Searching for Specific Music.

Double-tapping or double-clicking on the track number plays the song. It is that simple!

The **Playback Controls** are always visible at the bottom of the **Player Library** and their functions are similar to a normal CD player.

Burning CDs

With **Media Player** you can burn, or create, CD-R and CD-RW type CDs, as long as you have a suitable recorder on your PC. To begin, insert a blank CD into your disc drive. If the **AutoPlay** window pops up, choose **Burn an audio CD using Windows Media Player**. If not simply open Windows **Media Player** as usual.

Fig. 8.9 The Burn List Pane.

You burn a CD in the **Burn List** pane shown in Fig. 8.9. This should appear automatically, but if it doesn't just tap or click the **Burn** tab.

If there are items in the list, click **Clear list** to remove them. To name the new disc tap or click the **Burn list** item pointed to in Fig. 8.9, and type a name for it. This will show up on CD players that support CD text.

As with a **Playlist**, to add songs to the **Burn** list, find them in your **Player Library** and drag and drop them into the new list.

If necessary you next choose the **Disc Type** you want to burn. There are three different types of discs you can burn:

Audio CD – These hold about 80 minutes of music, are readable by computers and are playable in any CD player. This type was automatically selected in the example above.

Data CD – These hold about 700 MB of data, are readable by computers and CD players that support playback of digital audio files. They are not playable on standard CD players.

Data DVD – These hold about 4 GB of data and are readable by DVD players that support playback of digital audio files. They are primarily intended to be readable by computers. In Windows 8 & 8.1 you need to install **Media Center**.

To choose the type of disc to burn, click the **Burn options** button in the top right corner and choose from the drop-down menu. You can also adjust other options by clicking **More burn options** which opens the **Media Player Options** box shown below.

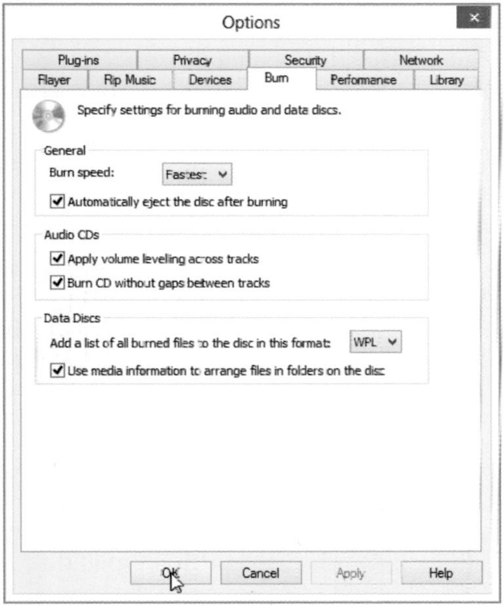

Fig. 8.10 Windows Media Player Options Box.

When you are happy with your settings, tap or click **Apply** and **OK**, followed by the **Start burn** button.

When the burn begins, the status is shown in a green bar at the top of the **Burn List**. Tapping or clicking the blue text link

below it lets you see the status of each individual track.

Quite a straightforward operation which you can use to create audio CDs to use in your car on those long boring journeys abroad!

Fig. 8.11 Burn Status.

Windows Media Center

Up to now, most people avoided using Windows **Media Center**, particularly since Windows **Media Player** used to serve their needs with playing films on DVDs. Not anymore!

With Windows 8.1 & 8, your DVD playback requires the use of **Media Center**, which you have to download and install on your computer as mentioned at the beginning of this chapter.

Windows **Media Center** is designed to serve as a home-entertainment hub for the living-room TV and was first included in various versions of pre-Windows 8, but with Windows 8 Pro and now Windows 8.1 Pro this is available as an add-on.

If you have a TV tuner for your computer, using Windows **Media Center** allows you to watch, pause, and record live TV, if not, there is still Internet TV which offers online shows and movies. But you can also use **Media Center** to play your videos and music and display your pictures from your computer's local hard drives, optical drives and from networks. It can then sort them by name, date, tags and other file attributes.

Adding and Installing Media Center

To download and add Windows **Media Center Pack** to Windows 8.1 Pro, swipe inwards from the right edge of the screen or point to the top-right corner of the screen with your mouse, then tap or click on the **Search** charm pointed to in the composite in Fig. 8.12, then:

- Enter **add media center to windows 8.1 Pro** in the text box and tap or click the **Search** button.

- Follow the information on the screen on how to download and install **Media Center**. Essentially you will need to:

  - Purchase a product key on line.

  - Download the **Media Center**.

  - Accept the license terms, before installation begins.

Fig. 8.12 Adding Features.

If you are running Windows 8.1 Pro, your computer will restart and Windows **Media Center** will be on it.

Note: If you are only running Windows 8.1 you will need to upgrade to Windows 8.1 Pro before you can install Media Center.

Starting Media Center

After installing Windows **Media Center**, you will find an additional tile on the **Start** screen, shown here. Tapping or clicking on this tile, starts Windows **Media Center**, as shown in Fig. 8.13 on the next page.

Fig. 8.13 A Media Center Screen.

Now, you might be forgiven if you don't know what to do next, but don't worry because you will soon come to grips with Windows **Media Center**. Normally the first screen you'll see is that of **Extras** shown at the very top of the screen in Fig. 8.13 above.

To move from one topic to another, either:

- Swipe upwards and when the required topic is under the focus (a kind of magnifying glass), swipe to the left to bring the options within this topic to the focus.

- Use the keyboard arrow keys; the down-arrow key moves the screen to the next topic, while the right-arrow key moves the screen to the next option within the selected topic.

The available topics are:

Extras   with options to   **extras library** and
                                              explore

Pictures + Videos	with options to	**picture library,** **play,** **favourites,** **radio** and **search**
Music	with options to	**music library,** **play favourites,** **radio** and **Search**
Movies	with options to	**movie library** and **play dvd**
TV	with options to	**recorded tv** and **live tv setup**
Tasks	with options to	**sync,** **add extender** and **media only**.

All you need to do here is try and see what is offered and soon you will realise what additions to your system are needed to get the most out of **Media Center**.

DVD Playback

The most important function for me is that of being able to play a DVD on my laptop. Just insert the DVD into the disc drive and **Media Center** starts playing almost straight away.

Fig. 8.14 Playing a DVD in Media Center.

Help and Support

It is left up to you to explore **Media Center's** other features listed on the previous page. At any time you can press the **F1** function key to get detailed **Help and Support** from Microsoft on topics such as how to connect your PC to your TV, how to connect your PC to a standard external monitor, keyboard and mouse, and how to stream your media over a home network to a **Media Center** extender.

Depending on your choice, you can watch and record live TV, create slide shows of your photos, listen to songs in your music library, and play CDs and DVDs. You could not ask for more. Have fun!

9

Some Useful Apps

There are several Apps which are new to Windows 8.1, such as **Health & Fitness**, **Food & Drink**, **Reading List**, **Alarms** and **Calculator**. Some of the new and some of the old Apps are covered in this chapter.

Health & Fitness

New to Windows 8.1 is the **Food & Drink** App. Its opening screen is similar to that in Fig. 9.1.

Fig. 9.1 The Health & Fitness Opening Screen.

As you can see, there is a lot of information to look at here. You could start by looking at the **Diet Tracker**, then **Nutrition and Calories**, before looking at the **Exercise Tracker**. I already feel very fit!

Food & Drink

Another new App is that of **Food & Drink**. After all that diet and exercise, you will be forgiven if you partake of something with more calories than you need! The opening screen of **Food & Drink** is similar to that in Fig. 9.2, similar because it very much depends on the season.

Fig. 9.2 The Food & Drink Opening Screen.

There goes all the effort of being healthy by watching your calorie intake and doing all the suggested exercises!

Having said that, do look at the options on the right panel which amongst other things, allows you to save a collection of recipes, create shopping lists or create a meal planner for individual days, as shown in Fig. 9.3.

Fig. 9.3 The Meal Planner Opening Screen.

The News App

These days every newspaper and other news source has a Web site showing a continuously updated online version of its news and story contents. We all like to know what is happening and where.

Windows 8.1 shows live content of news continuously as t happens as shown in Fig. 9.4 below.

Fig. 9.4 The Top Story in Today's News.

By the time you are reading this, the news would have changed, so a different picture will be displayed. Although it is possible to use **bing** to search for news, it is not as satisfying visually as using the **News** App, so it is not worth spending time on it.

News Layout

You can swipe to the left or use the right cursor key on the keyboard to see more sections under headings like **Top Stories**, **Our News Sources**, **World**, **Sci/Tech**, **Entertainment**, **Editor's Picks**, **Sport** and **Business**. In other words, everything to keep you occupied for quite a long time!

Each section has several topics within it, as shown in Fig. 9.5.

Fig. 9.5 Topics within a Section of Today's News.

Look on your screen to see when the last update was made which shows that you do get up-to-date news. When the mouse pointer passes over a topic, it highlights it indicating that if you tap or click, the full story of that topic will display.

Once a topic is selected, swiping upwards from the bottom of the screen or right-clicking, displays the options in Fig. 9.6.

Fig. 9.6 Options within Today's News.

The tools at the bottom of the screen, allow you to change the **Text style** and **size** or go to the **Previous** or **Next article**.

The Finance App

If you have a financial or business interest in company stocks and shares, mutual funds and international currency rates, then the **Finance** App will be useful to you. If not, you can probably skip the rest of this section. Windows 8.1's **bing Finance** offers an easy way to search for share prices, mutual fund details and financial information on publicly listed companies.

To access the **bing Finance** page, simply tap or click the **Finance** tile on the **Start** screen to open the first screen with the most recent news on finance, as shown in Fig. 9.7.

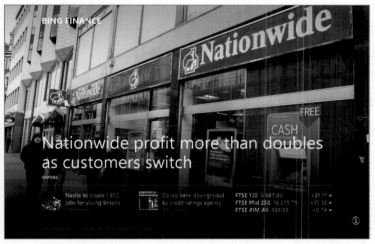

Fig. 9.7 Today's Bing Opening Finance Page.

The opening page should look similar to the one above, but obviously with different content. To the right of the page current topics under titles such as **Market**, **Watchlist**, **News** and **'Currencies' Across the Market**.

If you have obtained any quotes, these will be listed under **Watchlist**. Fig. 9.8 on the next page, displays what appears if you have not added to the list yet. You can add to or remove from the suggested list.

Fig. 9.8 Items on Watchlist.

To search for prices of mutual funds or stock market companies, first tap or click the **Add** ⊕ button to open the screen in Fig. 9.9. Next, use either their names or their ticker symbols and start typing. Bing is very clever here with its *Autosuggest* feature.

Fig. 9.9 Adding to the Watchlist.

As you type in the first part of a name a list instantly appears with suggestions on what you might be looking for, as shown in Fig. 9.10 below. You just tap or click the option you want in the list, the ticker symbol is automatically placed in the **Watchlist**, and the home page changes to a detailed page of data on the Company you searched for, as shown in Fig. 9.11 on the next page.

Add to Watchlist			
sai		×	
SAI	SAI Global Limited	Stock	Australia
SAI	Sunshine Agri-Tech, Inc.	Stock	TSX Ve...
SBRY	Sainsbury (J) PLC	Stock	London
0NWY	Saipem	Stock	London
0NWZ	Saipem	Stock	London

Fig. 9.10 Autosuggestion.

The contents of the above screen tend to be time-dependant, so you might see a different list for the same search criteria.

Company Summary

This gives an overview of the current UK financial situation of the selected company, with access to the main news story on the company displayed on the right of the screen of Fig. 9.11.

Fig. 9.11 SBRY Day Performance Chart.

Swiping to the left reveals screens which include summaries on **Key Statistics** and **Fund Ownership Trends**, as shown in Fig. 9.12 below.

Funds	Fund Rating	Buying/Selling Trend	% Change
CF TY Intl Equity (Ebias) A Acc	★★★★★	Buying	100.00%
AEGON Europees Mix Fonds	★★★★★	Selling	-99.85%
AEGON Wereldwijd Aandelen Fonds	★★★★★	Selling	-99.26%
Optimum Ibbotson Balanced Growth Plus	★★★★★	Buying	91.66%
Optimum Ibbotson Cons Gr Plus	★★★★★	Buying	86.35%
Legal and General - L&G CAF UK Equitrack	★★★★★	Buying	84.56%
Parworld Track UK	★★★★★	Selling	-81.96%
Smith & Williamson Enterprise Fund	★★★★★	Buying	80.00%
Smith & Williamson UK Equity Gr Trust	★★★★★	Buying	75.00%
JHVIT International Index Trust	★★★★★	Selling	-73.99%

SAINSBURY (J) PLC

FUND OWNERSHIP TRENDS

As compared to fund's last portfolio date

Fig. 9.12 Performance of Related Companies.

There is a lot more to this App, but I leave it to you to explore.

The Weather App

These days the weather is an integral part of news and finance. It certainly has a profound effect on both of these, so I decided to include it in this chapter.

Tapping or clicking the **Weather** App displays the following screen.

Fig. 9.13 The Weather at your Locality.

The **Weather** App allows you to customise it and include other localities, but to begin with it senses where you are, so what is displayed when you first start it is related to your area.

As you can see from the opening screen, there are additional screens which can be displayed by either swiping to the left or using the slider with the mouse. The slider only displays when your mouse pointer is placed near the bottom of the screen.

Additional tools can be displayed on the screen by swiping from the bottom edge of the screen upwards or right-clicking with the mouse. The usual tools appear at the bottom of the screen on the **Toolbar**, while at the top of the screen various options are displayed, as shown in Fig. 9.14 on the next page.

Fig. 9.14 The Weather Toolbar and Options.

On the top of the screen in Fig. 9.14, you can use the **Places** ⭐ button to open your **Favourites**. As you can see, I have already added an extra place by using the ⊚ button shown in

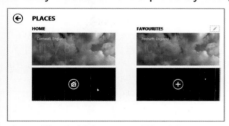

Fig. 9.15 Items on Watchlist.

Fig. 9.15. In fact, the buttons at the left of the **Toolbar** at the bottom of the screen only change to what appears in Fig. 9.14 after you have created an extra location.

Other **Toolbar** buttons can be used on selected sites to **Remove** them from **Favourites**, **Pin to Start** screen and even change displayed temperatures from Celsius to Fahrenheit.

A rather useful page in the **Weather** App gives you **Historical** information on monthly temperatures, rainfall and snow days, well worth examining these. Finally, if you are interested in **World Weather**, you can look at it from the comfort of your home by simply tapping or clicking the 🗺 button!

The Calculator App

There are two types of calculators, one for use with the **Desktop** view and another for the **Start** view. To find these, use the **Search** charm and type **calculator** in the **Search** box, as shown in Fig. 9.16, which returns two possibilities.

Fig. 9.16 Searching for an App.

The first **Calculator** is for use with the **Desktop**. Selecting it, displays the screen in Fig. 9.17 below with the **View** menu option selected so that you can see at a glance what is available.

Fig. 9.17 The Desktop App.

The second Calculator listed in Fig. 9.16 above is for use with the tiled **Start** screen. Selecting it, displays the full screen shown here in Fig. 9.18.

Apart from the usual **Standard** and **Scientific** modes, there is also a **Conversion** mode which should be of interest as it can convert various Imperial units to metric units. This should help with old recipes.

Fig. 9.18 The Start Screen App.

10

Connectivity & Mobility

Many homes and small offices these days have more than one PC and connecting to a network is a priority so that you can access the Internet from them all, share documents, pictures or music, and print to a single printer. Windows 8.1 makes this process very much easier than with pre-Windows 7 versions of the Operating System (OS), especially if all the computers are running under the same OS.

Joining a Network

 Although there are many types of networks, such as **Wireless**, **Ethernet**, **HomePNA** and **Powerline**, these days practically everybody uses **Wireless** (WiFi), so only this type of connection is covered here.

To set up a wireless network each computer to be included needs a **Wireless Network Adaptor**, which is built in these days in all laptops. You will also need a **Wireless Router** to allow access to the Internet and to 'connect' your networked computers.

Your Internet Service Provider (ISP) will often offer an ADSL or combination modem/wireless router as part of your Broadband package and some might even come and install it for you. Others might send you the necessary equipment and a CD to make the installation easier for you.

Once you have obtained and installed all this hardware you could, if you so wish, run the **Set up a new network** wizard from the main PC that is attached to the router.

To start the process of networking, use the **Search** charm and type **network** in the **Search** box, as shown in the composite screen dump in Fig. 10.1.

On the left half of the screen you can see a list of options for **Network** connections and settings. As an example, tap or click the **Connect to a network** option to display a screen similar to that in Fig. 10.2.

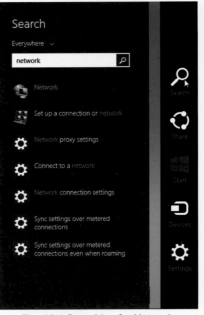

Fig. 10.1 Searching for Network Information.

Fig. 10.2 The Connections Screen.

The **Connections** screen that opens (Fig. 10.2) displays all the available WiFi networks near you. One of these is your own, if already configured and might already be connected, while the others belong to neighbours and normally require a key to join them. To open this screen in the future, tap or click on the **Network** icon on the right side of the **Taskbar**, 🖫 or ⏹.

I suggest you have a look at the other **Network** settings in Fig. 10.1, before you try to set up a new connection.

To set up a new connection you tap or click the **Set up a connection or network** which displays Fig. 10.3.

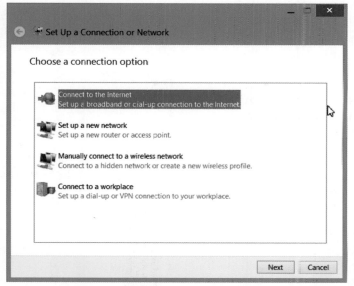

Fig. 10.3 The Network and Sharing Center.

To continue, tap or click the **Set up a new network – Set up a new router or access point** option. You will be stepped through the process of adding other computers and devices to the network.

Network Connection

With Windows 8.1 if a computer has a working network adaptor, the **Network** icon appears in the **Notification** area at the right end of the **Taskbar**. This icon indicates whether your network adaptor is an **Ethernet** 🖳 adaptor or a wireless ᴬᴵᴵ adaptor with bars indicating the signal strength, 5 being the strongest. When the computer is not connected to a network, an **x** shows on the connection 🖳 icon, whereas while it is connecting it shows as 🖳. When a wireless connection is not available, the icon has a 🖳 starburst.

When you physically connect your computer to a network with an **Ethernet** cable, Windows 8.1 automatically creates the network connection, but to connect to a wireless network for the first time, you might need select your Broadband

connection and make the connection yourself by tapping or clicking the **Connect automatically** box to select it, followed by the **Connect** button that displays, as shown in Fig. 10.4.

Fig. 10.4 Connecting to a Network.

If a **WEP** key or **WPA** password is required, you will be prompted to enter it, and then Windows will connect to the selected network.

Wireless Network Security

For very obvious reasons, when you set up a wireless network you should set it up so that only people you choose can access it. There are several wireless network security systems available:

WPA (Wi-Fi Protected Access) encrypts information, checks to make sure that the network security key has not been modified and also authenticates users to help ensure that only authorised people can access the network.

WEP (Wired Equivalent Privacy) is an older network security method that is still available to support older devices. It uses a network security key which encrypts the information sent across your network. However, WEP security is relatively easy to break and is not recommended on its own.

Also 802.1x authentication can help enhance security for 802.11 type wireless networks and wired **Ethernet** networks. It can work with **WPA** or **WEP** keys and uses an authentication server to validate users and provide network access. This is used mainly in company networks.

HomeGroup

The easiest way of getting to **HomeGroup** is via the **Control Panel**. To do this, first activate the **Desktop Internet Explorer** bring up the **Charms** bar, tap or click on the **Settings** charm and select **Control Panel**, as shown in the composite in Fig. 10.5.

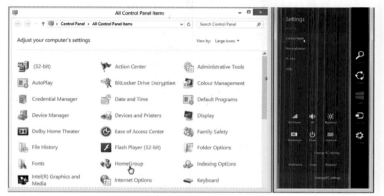

Fig. 10.5 The HomeGroup Control Panel Link.

This feature simplifies the whole network procedure, particularly when the networked PCs are running under Windows 8.1.

Tapping or clicking the **HomeGroup** link, opens a screen in which you are told that there is a **HomeGroup** available on the network. Using the **Join now** button starts the process. In the next screen, select what libraries and devices you want to share and tap or click the **Next** button, then tap or click **Next** followed by **Finish** to complete the process.

You have to repeat this procedure to add all your other computers on your home network to the **HomeGroup**. Quite a tedious operation, but it doesn't take long and in the end is well worth the trouble.

> **Note:** It is important to restart the computers for these changes to take effect.

All your Windows 8.1 computers in the same **HomeGroup** can share libraries, folders, files, devices and media without ever having to type passwords whenever anything is accessed. You select what you want shared on each computer and as long as it is 'awake' it can be accessed from the other computers in the group with just a few taps or clicks. You can even change what is shared, as shown in Fig. 10. 6.

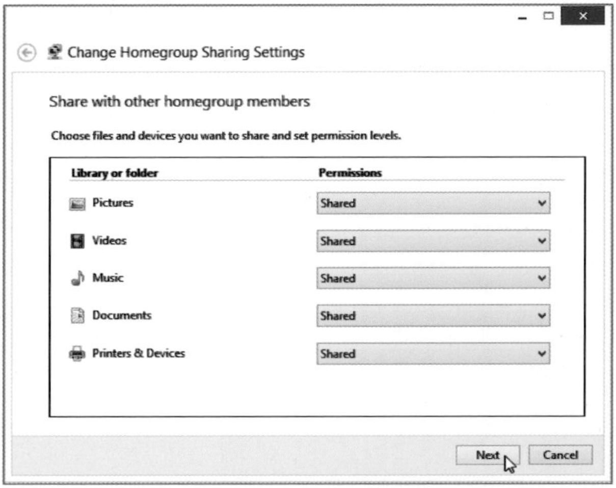

Fig. 10.6 Changing HomeGroup Permissions.

Now select what you want to share from a list of your default libraries (**Pictures**, **Videos**, **Music** and **Documents**) and your printers. Having done so, tap or click on **Next**.

Accessing HomeGroup Computers

Once the **HomeGroup** is created and all your home computers are joined, accessing their shared libraries is very easy. Just open up **File Explorer** and tap or click on **Homegroup** in the **Navigation** pane. In Fig. 10.7, you see the computers that are turned on and are not in sleep mode.

Fig. 10.7 The Homegroup.

The STUDYPC is the computer I am on right now, while NOELSLAPTOP is a computer on the network and I can access all its libraries. Tapping or clicking on a library will open up all the folders and files in it. Very quick and easy.

Sharing Printers

To share printers on your network, even if they are not in a **HomeGroup**, so everyone in your household can connect as long as the printers and PCs are switched on you do as follows. On the computer that the printer is attached to, tap or click the **Desktop** tile, then activate the **Charms** bar and select the **Settings** charm and tap or click on **Control Panel**.

On the **Control Panel** tap or click the **Devices and Printers** link to open the **Devices and Printers** window, locate the printer attached to the computer, touch and hold or right-click and select **Set as default printer** from the displayed drop-down menu.

For the same printer, touch and hold or right-click and select **Printer properties** from the displayed drop-down menu to open the **Properties** dialogue box, then tap or click the **Sharing** tab, and tap or click the Change Sharing Options button and tap or click the **Share this printer** box to select it, then press **OK** to approve the options and close the **Properties** dialogue box.

Before you can use a shared printer from your other computers on the network, you have to add it to the list of available printers on each of the PCs by opening the **Devices and Printers** window and selecting the Add a printer button and selecting your printer from the list that displays. Wait for the printer driver to be located and loaded. Now any computer on the network can select the printer and use it just as if it were directly connected to it, but it requires the PC which is connected to the printer to be on.

> **Note:** If you had a wireless printer, it would be detected by all the computers on the network, which greatly simplifies sharing a printer.

Mobility

By mobility I am referring here to computer mobility, not your ability to get around! One of the nice things about using Windows 8.1 on a **mobile** notebook or netbook PC is that the most important configuration options are consolidated into a single utility, the **Windows Mobility Center**. This is where you should go when you want to control how your mobile PC works.

Windows Mobility Center

To launch the **Mobility Center**, tap or click the **Desktop** tile in the **Start** screen, then activate the **Charms** bar. Next, tap or click the **Settings** charm, and select **Control Panel**.

At nearly the very end of the **Control Panel** list, you will find the **Windows Mobility Center** link shown here. Tapping or clicking on this link, opens a window like the one in Fig. 10.8 below.

Fig. 10.8 Windows Mobility Center for a Laptop.

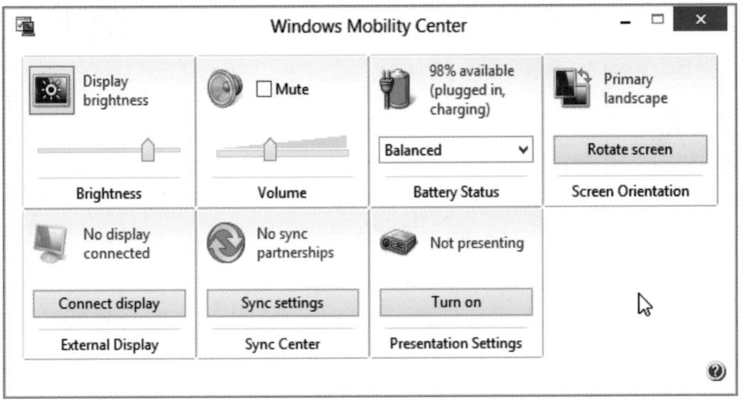

The **Mobility Center** includes panels for the most common laptop settings. These are:

Brightness

Display brightness

A slider temporarily adjusts the display brightness. If you hover the mouse over the display icon it turns into a button which opens the **Power Options** window, where you can change the brightness level on your current power plan.

Volume

 ☐ Mute

Adjusts the volume level of your computer's sound and lets you mute it. Tap or click the speaker graphic to open the **Sound** dialogue box where you can adjust all the audio settings on your laptop.

Battery Status

Displays the current charge status of your computer's battery and lets you change the power plan. Tap or click the battery graphic, to open the **Power Options** window where you can edit the power plans and create your own custom power plans, as discussed in the next section.

Screen Orientation

Primary landscape

Displays the orientation of your screen. Tap or click the screen graphic to open the **Screen Resolution** panel, where you can change the appearance of your display.

External Display

No display connected

Lets you connect your laptop to an external monitor or projector. Tap or click the display graphic to open the **Screen Resolution** window where you can change the resolution and orientation of both your internal and external displays.

Tap or click the **Connect display** button to open the options available for projecting to a secondary screen.

Sync Center

Lets you check the results of your recent synchronisation activity if you've set up your computer to sync files with a network server.

All in all this is a very useful facility for mobile users. Some notebook manufacturers might include their own panels.

Note: The **Mobility Center** by default, is only available on laptops, netbooks, and tablet PCs. It is not available on desktop computers unless it is enabled.

Power Plans

If you are worried when using a laptop away from the mains about how much power it is using, then read on as even the best batteries seem to run low far too quickly!

As well as the **Battery Status** tile in the **Mobility Center**, the battery meter in the **Notification** area of the **Taskbar** shows you the state of your laptop's battery. If you hover over it, the % charge appears. If you tap it or click it, a pop-up like that in Fig. 10.9 opens showing what power plan is active.

Fig. 10.9 Battery Status.

The Windows 8 **Power Plans** cater for three main power designs that can help you save energy, maximise system performance, or achieve a balance between the two. To see the default power plans, tap or click the **More power options** link in the above pop-up to open the **Power Options** window shown in Fig. 10.10 on the next page.

You can also open the **Power Options** window from the **Battery Status** tile in the **Mobility Center**, or by tapping or clicking the **Power Options** link in the **Control Panel**.

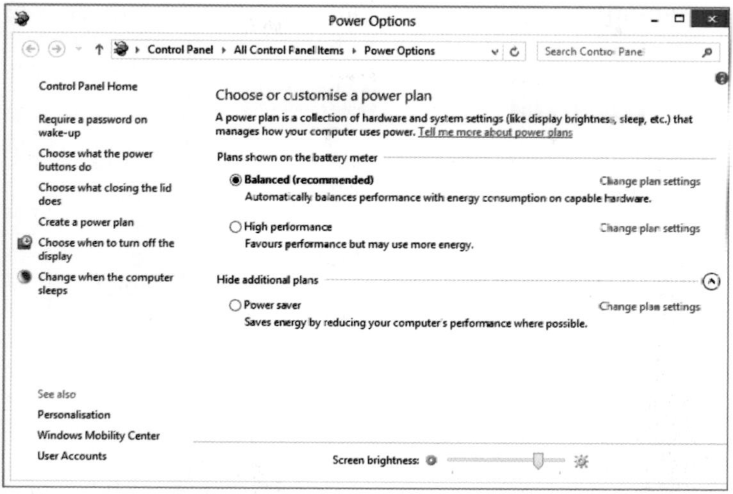

Fig. 10.10 The Power Options Window.

The three default **Power Plans** are:

Balanced – Giving good performance when it is needed. but saving power during periods of inactivity.

High performance – Giving maximum brightness and performance, but using far more power, making it rather unhelpful to mobile users unless they are plugged in to the mains.

Power saver – Saves power by reducing screen brightness and system performance. This can be useful if you are ever 'caught out'.

Which plan to use? For most people much of the time the default **Balanced** plan is a good compromise between battery life and performance. Many people will never change it from the recommended option.

When you are away from home and operating on batteries the **Power saver** plan will probably give you a few more minutes of battery life, but do remember to reduce display brightness as this uses more power than any other part of a computer. Also disconnect devices that you are not actually using, such as USB devices which use power just by being connected.

You should only really use the **High performance** plan when you are connected to mains power and have a full battery charge.

These three power plans should meet your needs most of the time, but if you want to build your own, then you can use one of the default power plans as a starting point. All of them can be adapted by clicking on their **Change plan settings** link in the **Power Options** window. The main settings in the **Edit Plan Settings** windows that open are when to **Turn off the display**, and when to **Put the computer to sleep**. But the **Change advanced power settings** link gives you almost absolute control over everything, as shown in Fig. 10.11.

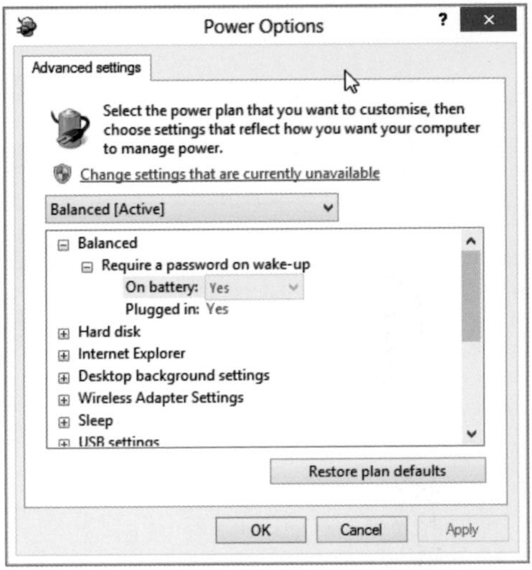

Fig. 10.11 Changing Advanced Power Settings.

You do have lots of option to examine and think about their effect, so spending some time here might be worthwhile.

11

Accessibility

The Ease of Access Center

If you have problems using a standard computer Windows 8 has several features that may be of help.

 The **Ease of Access Center** lets you change settings to make your PC more accessible if you have visual or hearing difficulties, suffer pain in your hands or arms and/or have other reasoning and cognitive issues.

You can open the **Ease of Access Center** by using the **Settings** charm, then selecting **Control Panel** and tapping or clicking the **Ease of Access Center**, as shown in the composite screen dump in Fig. 11.1.

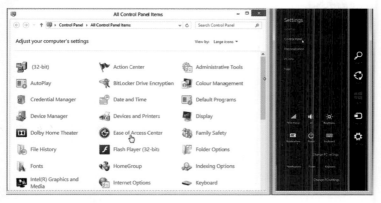

Fig. 11.1 The Ease of Access Center Entry in the Control Panel.

However, an easier way to open the **Ease of Access Center**, if you have a keyboard, is by using the ⊞+U keyboard shortcut (where ⊞ is the Windows keyboard key).

Both methods open the screen shown in Fig. 11.2 below.

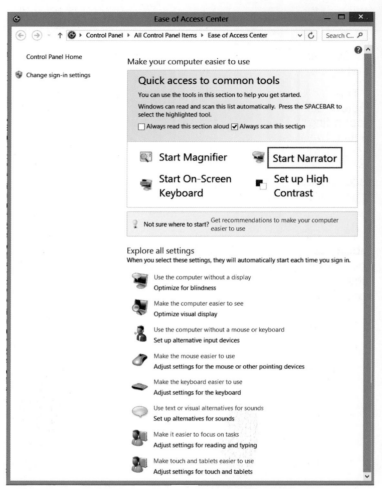

Fig. 11.2 The Ease of Access Center Screen.

The **Ease of Access Center** includes a quick access panel at the top with a highlight rotating through the four most common tools; **Start Magnifier**, **Start Narrator**, **Start On-Screen Keyboard**, and **Set up High Contrast**. A voice, the Narrator, also tells you what option is selected.

Pressing the **Spacebar** on a highlighted option will start that option. If the Narrator annoys you, click the **Always read this section aloud** box to remove the tick mark from it. While you are doing this, you could also remove the tick mark from the **Always scan this section** box, to stop the focus from rotating between the four entries.

The 💡 **Get recommendations to make your computer easier to use** link opens a five-stage questionnaire. Depending on your answers to questions about performing routine tasks, such as whether you have difficulty seeing faces or text on TV, hearing conversations, or using a pen or pencil, Windows will provide a recommendation of the accessibility settings and programs that are likely to improve your ability to see, hear and use your computer. This has to be a good place to start.

The **Explore all settings** section below the **Get recommendations ...** link in the **Ease of Access Center** lets you explore settings options by categories. When selected, these will automatically start each time you log on to the computer. They include:

- Using the computer without a display

- Making the computer easier to see

- Using the computer without a mouse or keyboard

- Making a mouse easier to use

- Making the keyboard easier to use

- Using text or visual alternatives for sounds

- Making it easier to focus on tasks

- Making touch and tablets easier to use.

In the next few pages I will give you an overview of these various options, but I will not discuss any of them in too much detail, as different people have different and specific needs!

The Microsoft Magnifier

To start the **Magnifier**, click on **Start Magnifier** (words not icon) shown in Fig. 11.3.

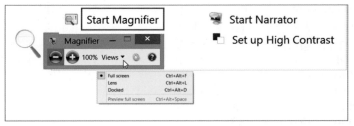

Fig. 11.3 Computer Screen with the Magnifier Active.

The new **Magnifier** window has two views: **Full screen** (the default), and **Lens**, selected from the **Views** drop-down list shown open in the composite screen dump in Fig. 11.3.

In **Lens** view, wherever you place the mouse pointer the screen is magnified.

The **Magnifier** window allows you to increase 🔵 or decrease ⊖ the magnification, or use the **Options** icon 🔅 to turn on colour inversion, select tracking options and fine-tune screen fonts.

If you don't use the **Magnifier** window for more than a few seconds, it turns into an actual magnifying glass icon, as shown here. Clicking this **Magnifier** icon again, re-opens the **Magnifier** window shown in Fig. 11.3 above.

To close down the **Magnifier**, click the **Close** button in the **Magnifier** window.

This feature takes a while to get used to, but it can be well worthwhile trying it out.

Microsoft Narrator

Narrator is a basic screen reader built into Windows and may be useful for the visually impaired. It reads dialogue boxes and window controls in a number of Windows basic applications, as long as the computer being used has a sound card and speakers or headphones.

To open the **Narator**, tap or click the **Start Narrator** option in the **Ease of Access Center** (Fig. 11.2). Another way to start **Narrator** is to use the key combination **🚩+Enter**. **Narrator** will start speaking in a rather hard to understand electronic voice reading everything that you point at with the mouse pointer.

After starting **Narrator**, an icon is placed on the **Task** bar. Clicking that icon opens the **Narrator Settings** screen in which you can:

- Change how **Narrator** starts

- Change how you interact with your PC

- Change the pitch or volume of the current voice or choose an alternative voice.

Finally, it might be worth visiting the **Narrator** keyboard commands screen to find out what commands are available to control **Narrator**. You do this by using the key combination **CapsLock+F1**. On the screen that opens, you'll find both keyboard commands and touch commands to completely control **Narrator**. While you are looking at these commands, you can stop **Narrator** from going on reading one command after another, by pressing the **Ctrl** key.

If you find this **Narrator** useful you will need to play around with it for a while until you get familiar with the way it works.

To close **Narrator** just use the key combination **CapsLock+Esc** and click **Yes** on the warning box that displays. **Narrator** even tells you that you are on the **Yes** button just before it closes down!

The On-Screen Keyboard

To activate the **On-Screen Keyboard** (Fig. 11.4), click the **Start On-Screen Keyboard** option in the **Ease of Access Center** shown earlier in Fig. 11.2.

Fig. 11.4 The On-Screen Keyboard.

This excellent virtual keyboard opens on the screen and allows users with mobility impairments to type data using a mouse pointer, a joystick, or other pointing device. The result is exactly as if you were using the actual keyboard. It has three typing modes selected when the **Options** key on the virtual keyboard is tapped or clicked.

The three modes of the virtual keyboard are:

Click on keys mode – you tap or click the on-screen keys to type text (the default mode).

Hover over keys mode – you use a finger, a mouse or joystick to point to a key for a predefined period of time, and the selected character is typed automatically.

Scan through keys mode – the **On-Screen Keyboard** continually scans the keyboard and highlights areas where you can type keyboard characters by pressing a hot key or using a switch-input device.

You can also adjust the settings for your 'physical' keyboard by clicking the ⬤ **Make the keyboard easier to use** entry towards the middle of the **Ease of Access Center** window (see Fig. 11.2), and selecting various options on a displayed window.

On the 'Make the keyboard easier to use screen' you can:

Turn on Mouse Keys – lets you move the mouse pointer by pressing the arrow keys on the keyboard's numeric pad.

Turn on Sticky Keys – allows you to press the **Ctrl**, **Alt**, and **Shift**, keys one at a time, instead of all at the same time. This is useful for people who have difficulty pressing two or more keys at a time.

Turn on Toggle Keys – makes your computer play a high-pitched sound when the **Caps Lock**, **Scroll Lock**, or **Num Lock** keys are used. The **Turn on Filter Keys** option tells the keyboard to ignore brief or repeated keystrokes.

The Display Options

To make your screen easier to see you can try the **Set up High Contrast** option in Fig. 11.2. This opens yet another window in which you can set programs to change their colour-specific schemes to a **High Contrast** scheme, change the size of text, set the thickness of the blinking cursor, etc.

The Mouse Options

Clicking the 🖰 **Make the mouse easier to use** link near the middle of Fig. 11.2, displays the window shown in Fig. 11.5 on the next page.

In that screen you can change the colour and size of the mouse pointer, and control the mouse pointer's movements with the keys on the numeric keypad.

Tapping or clicking the **Set up Mouse Keys** link, pointed to in Fig. 11.5, displays an additional window in which you can control, amongst other things, the speed at which the mouse pointer moves, and the shortcut key combination you need to activate and deactivate the numeric keypad.

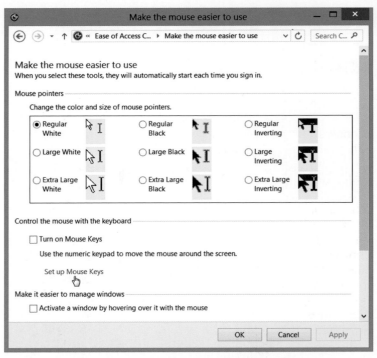

Fig. 11.5 Making the Mouse Easier to Use.

I'll leave it to you to explore the other settings on the list in the lower half of the **Ease of Access Center**. It is the only way of finding out what suits you personally.

12

Looking After Your PC

Windows 8.1 comes equipped with a full range of utilities for you to easily maintain your PC's health and well being. You can access some of these tools by tapping or clicking the **Desktop** tile in the **Start** menu, selecting the **Settings Charm** from the **Charms** bar, then tapping or clicking the **PC info** option listed under **Settings** and pointed to in Fig. 12.1. This opens the **System Information** screen shown in Fig. 12.2.

Fig. 12.1 Settings Options.

Fig. 12.2 System Information Screen.

This is the easiest to take a first look at – it displays such things as your Operating System, System Summary, Hardware Resources, etc. However, each computer is bound to be different, so don't expect to see the same information, but what is important here are the links at the left of the screen which deal with prevention of system problems.

Problem Prevention

Windows has strong protection against **System** corruption:

* System Protection
* System Restore
* Automatic Update

Each of these will be discussed separately.

System Protection

Windows applications sometimes can, and do, overwrite important **System** files. Windows 8.1 protects your **System** files by automatically saving them at regular intervals, but you must check the settings and if necessary change them.

The first setting to be checked is the **System Protection**. To do this, tap or click the **System protection** link at the top-left corner in Fig. 12.2 to open the tabbed dialogue box shown in Fig. 12.3.

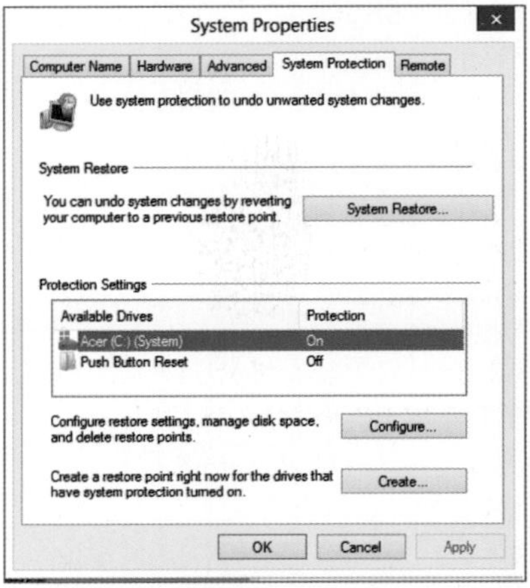

Fig. 12.3 System Protection Tab.

With the **System Protection** tab selected, check that the C: drive (the one that Windows 8.1 is installed on), under **Protection Settings** in Fig. 12.3, is **On**.

If not, select the option, then tap or click the **Configure** button and tap or click the **Turn on system protection** radio button on the displayed screen to select it. Next, move the slider next to **Max Usage** to, say, 2% to indicate the maximum disc space to be used for system protection and tap or click **Apply**, followed by **OK**.

This returns you to the dialogue box of Fig. 12.3 where you should tap or click the **Create** button to create a restore point right now. On the dialogue box that opens, give the restore point a descriptive name, and tap or click **Create**.

In the future, you can undo system changes by reverting your PC to the state it was when you created the restore point. This is done by activating the **System Restore** button in Fig. 12.3 which starts the **System Restore** Wizard. Tapping or clicking **Next** displays a dialogue box with all your **Restore** points for you to choose from.

Restore points are created automatically by the system every time you install or uninstall a program. This is a precaution just in case a newly installed program creates problems, so you can revert back to the state the computer was in prior to the installation that caused the problem. This is an excellent protection of your system.

Automatic Update

Windows can automatically update any **System** files as they become available from Microsoft's Web site. To make sure this happens, click the **Windows Update** link at the bottom-left corner in Fig. 12.2. This displays a screen from where you can connect to Microsoft's Web site to see if there are any updates available.

The system is normally set to automatically install updates. If that is not the case, you can use the **Change settings** link to do so. This is important as it guarantees that you are always up to date, as possible security issues that are found and corrected by Microsoft are installed on your system straight away.

System and Security

To examine the other options in the Windows **System and Security center**, tap or click the **Desktop** tile on the **Start** screen, then use the **Settings** charm and select **Control Panel**. Next, choose to **View by: Category**, and click the **System and Security** icon, shown here, to display the window shown in Fig. 12.4.

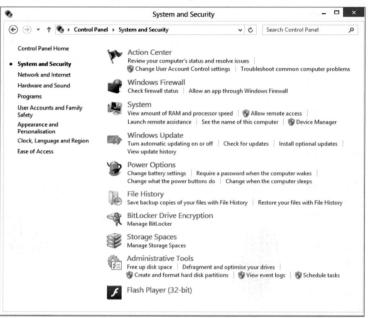

Fig. 12.4 The Windows System and Security Screen.

Action Center

The **Action Center** looks after message alerts from key Windows security and maintenance features. When Windows requires your attention, the **Action Center** icon appears in the **Taskbar**. Tapping or clicking this icon opens a pop-up box which lists the problems and gives suggested fixes for them. You can then tap or click a solution to solve a problem.

Windows Firewall

For your PC to be secure, make sure that the Windows **Firewall** is switched on. Tapping or clicking the **Check firewall status**

link in Fig. 12.4, shown here enlarged, displays a screen in which you can change the **Firewall** settings.

A **Firewall** is a software security system that sits between your computer and the outside world and is used to set restrictions on what information is passed to and from the Internet. In other words it protects you from uninvited access.

If your **Firewall** is turned off, or you do not have up-to-date virus protection, the **Action Center** will flag an error by placing the 🔳 icon in the **Notification** area of the **Taskbar**.

Hard Disc Management

There are two Apps in Windows 8.1 to help you keep your hard disc in good condition: **Disk Clean-up**, which removes unnecessary files from your hard disc and frees up space, and **Defragment and Optimise Drives** which optimises your hard discs by rearranging their data to eliminate unused spaces, which speeds up access to your hard discs.

Disk Clean-up

The best way of accessing these tools is via the **Administrative Tools** in Fig. 12.4 on previous page and shown here enlarged.

Fig. 12.5.

Tapping or clicking the **Free up disk space** link, starts the **Disk Clean-up** program which scans your hard disc, then lists temporary files, Internet cache files, and other files that you can safely delete. You should carry out this operation at least once a week.

Defragmenting Hard Discs

To start **Disk Defragmenter**, tap or click the **Defragment and optimise drives** link in Fig. 12.5 on previous page.

The **Disk Defragmenter** optimises your hard discs by rearranging their data to eliminate unused spaces, which speeds up access by all Windows and other program operations. You should run this program at least once a month.

Backing Up Your Data

Anyone can lose files by either accidentally deleting or replacing them, a virus attack, or a software or hardware failure, such as a complete hard disc failure. With Windows, you can use **System Restore** to recover your system files, you can reinstall your programs, but not your precious data files or pictures and videos of your family. To protect these, you should regularly create backups. Windows makes backing up easy, and has a range of features to seamlessly protect your data and system setup.

Backing Up and Restoring Files

Windows 8.1 allows you to back up your data files and recover them later. To find the applications that do this, activate the **Charms** bar and type **data backup** in the **Search** box. What is found is shown in Fig. 12.6.

Fig. 12.6 Locating File History Applications.

You can save your data files to either an external USB drive or to **SkyDrive**. This is up to you, but having started the process, be patient, especially if this is the first time you are saving your files. What will be saved are all the **Libraries**, the **Desktop**, all your **Contacts**, **Favourites** and all the files on your **SkyDrive**.

Once you create the initial backup, you really never have to think about backing up your files again since Windows will regularly do this for you according to the schedule you set. Do read the information on screen and change any suggestions you don't like.

Restoring files and folders from your backups is very easy. There can be several backups (depending on the frequency of backing up your data in **Advanced Settings**), from which to make a choice. You do this by selecting the first option of the search results, in Fig. 12.6 which displays all your backups for you to choose from.

If you need to make an 'image backup' of your whole drive, meaning everything on your hard drive, Windows **System** files, all your additional installed programs and all your data, then you have to resort to programs specifically design for the purpose. A quick search on the Internet should reveal a host of such programs, but make quite sure that the one you choose is compatible with Windows 8.1 (many are not)!

Windows Defender

Windows **Defender** is free anti-spyware software that can be downloaded from:

www.windowsdefender.com

Windows **Defender** helps protect your computer against spyware and other potentially dangerous software being installed on your computer when you are connected to the Internet. It offers two ways to help keep infections at bay:

- In real-time, it alerts you when spyware attempts to install itself on your computer, tries to run on it, or attempts to change Windows settings.

- At any time, you can scan for spyware that might be installed on your computer, having bypassed Windows **Defender**, and automatically remove them and the problems they may cause.

To open Windows **Defender**, action the **Charms** bar, select **Settings**, then **Control Panel**. Near the bottom of the displayed list of options (viewed in **Large icons**), tap/click the option shown here. This opens a screen similar to that shown in Fig. 12.7, provided the **Defender** is turned on. If it is not, you may get a message asking you to do so.

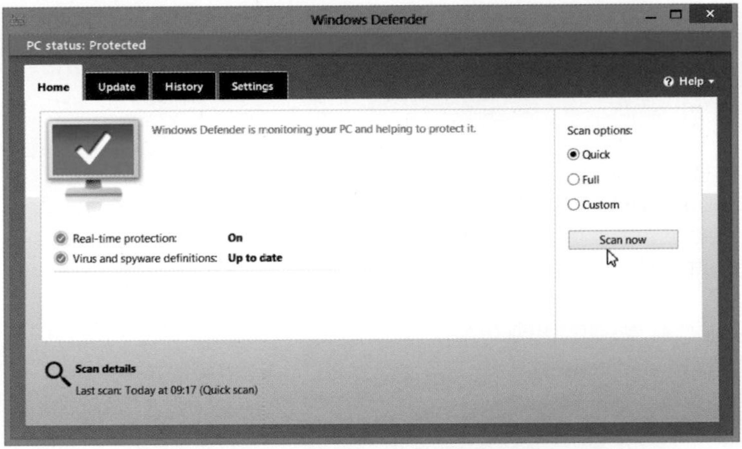

Fig. 12.7 The Defender's PC Status Screen.

As you can see, in my case the **Defender** is turned on and the **PC Status** is **Protected**. However, the first time the **Defender** is opened, you will get a window in which you'll be asked to **Check for new definitions**. It is very important to have up-to-date 'definitions', or files listing potential software threats. Once it is switched on, the program will work with Windows **Update** to automatically install new definitions.

Windows **Defender** offers three types of scan: (a) **Quick** (the default) which checks the most likely places on your hard disc that spyware will be located, (b) **Full** which checks all your files and all currently running programs and (c) **Custom** which allows you to select which partition, hard drive or attached drives to scan.

For more in-depth information, look at Windows **Defender Help**, accessed by clicking the ❷ button in Fig. 12.7.

Windows Firewall

For your PC to be secure, make sure that the Windows **Firewall** is switched on. Tapping or clicking the **Check**

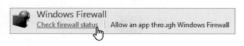

firewall status link in Fig. 12 4, shown here enlarged, displays a screen in which you can change the **Firewall** settings.

A **Firewall** is a software security system that sits between your computer and the outside world and is used to set restrictions on what information is passed to and from the Internet. In other words it protects you from uninvited access.

If your **Firewall** is turned off, or you do not have up-to-date virus protection, the **Action Center** will flag an error by placing the 🗗 icon in the **Notification** area of the **Taskbar**.

Hard Disc Management

There are two Apps in Windows 8.1 to help you keep your hard disc in good condition: **Disk Clean-up**, which removes unnecessary files from your hard disc and frees up space, and **Defragment and Optimise Drives** which optimises your hard discs by rearranging their data to eliminate unused spaces, which speeds up access to your hard discs.

Disk Clean-up

The best way of accessing these tools is via the **Administrative Tools** in Fig. 12.4 on previous page and shown here enlarged.

Fig. 12.5.

Tapping or clicking the **Free up disk space** link, starts the **Disk Clean-up** program which scans your hard disc, then lists temporary files, Internet cache files, and other files that you can safely delete. You should carry out this operation at least once a week.

Defragmenting Hard Discs

To start **Disk Defragmenter**, tap or click the **Defragment and optimise drives** link in Fig. 12.5 on previous page.

The **Disk Defragmenter** optimises your hard discs by rearranging their data to eliminate unused spaces, which speeds up access by all Windows and other program operations. You should run this program at least once a month.

Backing Up Your Data

 Anyone can lose files by either accidentally deleting or replacing them, a virus attack, or a software or hardware failure, such as a complete hard disc failure. With Windows, you can use **System Restore** to recover your system files, you can reinstall your programs, but not your precious data files or pictures and videos of your family. To protect these, you should regularly create backups. Windows makes backing up easy, and has a range of features to seamlessly protect your data and system setup.

Backing Up and Restoring Files

Windows 8.1 allows you to back up your data files and recover them later. To find the applications that do this, activate the **Charms** bar and type **data backup** in the **Search** box. What is found is shown in Fig. 12.6.

Results for "data backup"

Restore your files with File History

Save **backup** copies of your files with File History

Fig. 12.6 Locating File History Applications.

You can save your data files to either an external USB drive or to **SkyDrive**. This is up to you, but having started the process, be patient, especially if this is the first time you are saving your files. What will be saved are all the **Libraries**, the **Desktop**, all your **Contacts**, **Favourites** and all the files on your **SkyDrive**.

Appendix A

Controlling Windows 8.1

Windows 8.1 functions are at their best when you learn to use the charms and finger gestures so that you can quickly jump between the **Desktop** screen and the **Start** screen, or your own programs and the new Windows Apps.

Below you will find a list of the most useful Windows 8 touch controls and their mouse and keyboard equivalents, together with appropriate screens illustrating various methods.

Displaying the Charms Bar

- Touch Control – Swipe with your thumb to the left from the right edge of the screen.

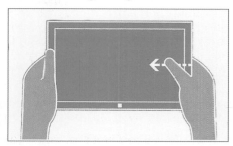

Fig. A.1 How to Hold a Touch Screen.

- Mouse Control – Move mouse pointer to the top-right or bottom-right corner of the screen.

- Keyboard Control – Press simultaneously the two keys ⊞+C (where ⊞ is the Windows key on your keyboard).

Zooming In or Out

- Touch Control – Place two fingers on the screen and push them apart to zoom in; pinch two fingers together to zoom out.

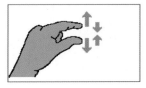

Fig. A.2 Using Fingers to Zoom In or Out.

- Mouse Control – Hold the **Ctrl** key down and use the scroll wheel on the mouse to zoom in and out.

Closing Running Apps

- Touch Control – Drag a finger from the top edge of the screen towards the bottom edge until the App minimises and disappears.

- Mouse Control – Move the mouse pointer to the top edge of the screen and when it changes to an open hand, then click and drag towards the bottom edge of the screen until the App minimises and disappears.

- Keyboard Control – Press simultaneously the two keys **Alt+F4**.

Fig. A.3 Closing a Running App.

Index

A

Accessibility........... 155
Accessing HomeGroup. 148
Account
    Administrator......... 32
    Mail................. 71
    Microsoft............. 33
    SkyDrive............. 47
Action Center....... 19, 166
Active window.......... 38
Add to Favourites....... 61
Address bar. 53, 57, 87, 124
Adjust screen resolution. . 27
Administrator........... 32
Album Info............ 121
Anti-spyware software. . 169
Anti-virus software...... 4, 5
Attachment (Mail)....... 77
Audio CD ripping....... 123
Autocomplete button..... 57
Automatic Update...... 165
Autoplay window....... 126
AVG protection........... 5

B

Back up (Data)......... 168
Background...... 7, 22, 106
Backup
    Restore............. 168
Battery status.......... 151
Bing
    Environment.......... 87
    Finance............. 137
    Help................ 70

Maps................ 87
Maps App........... 103
Navigation bar........ 87
Search preferences... 54
Bird's eye map... 87, 89, 91
Bookmarks............. 62
Boot-up Process........ 29
Brightness control...... 151
Broadband... 4, 74, 87, 143
Browsing
    History............... 63
    InPrivate............. 65
    Tabbed.............. 65
Burn CD..... 106, 120, 126

C

Calculator App......... 142
Calendar App........... 85
Camera (get photos).... 110
Category view......... 166
CD
    Burn................ 126
    Play................ 120
    Rip button........... 123
Change
    Active window........ 41
    Date and Time........ 15
    PC settings........... 25
    Program............. 31
    Search engine........ 67
Charms Bar........ 20, 171
Check Updates........ 165
Clean installation......... 2
Cleanup (disc)......... 167

Clock. 15, 19
Close
   Button. 37
   Running Apps. 172
   Window. 37
Collage (photos). 111
Command bar (Bing). 60
Compatibility
   Mode. 59
   View button. 59
Configure printer. 29
Connecting
   to Network. 143
   to Server. 71
Contacts. 81, 168
Contextual
   Menu. 106
   Tabs. 44
Control
   Devices and Printers. . 28
   Panel. 112, 147, 156, 166
Controls
   Navigation. 93
   Playback. 124, 126
   Viewer. 107
Create
   Folder on SkyDrive. . . . 48
   New folder 37, 44, 48, 109
   User accounts. 21

D
Data (Back up). 168
Date (change). 15
Default printer. . 30, 113, 149
Defender (Windows). . . . 169
Defragment hard disc. . . 168
Delete
   Command. 44
   Message. 78

Desktop
   Bing environment. 87
   Media Player. 119
   Music Library. 117
   Pictures Library. 83
   SkyDrive. 47
   Tile. 14
   Video Library. 115
   View. 7, 10
Details pane. 37, 123
Devices control. 28
Directions link (Bing). 94
Disc
   Defragmenting. 168
   Management. 167
Disk Clean-up. 167
Display
   Change. 27
   Charms bar. 20, 171
   Options. 161
Document sharing. 143
Draft folder (Mail). . . . 72, 79
Drag and Drop. 51, 126
DVD play. 117, 127, 131

E
Ease of Access Center. . 155
Edit
   Contacts. 83
   E-mail. 75, 78
   Pictures. 77
E-mail
   App. 71
   Attachment. 75
Ethernet. 19, 143
Exit Explorer. 56
Expand Ribbon. 37, 43
Explorer (Internet)
   Buttons. 57

Command bar........ 60
Help................ 69
Menu bar............ 40
Private Browsing...... 65
Toolbars............. 58
External Display........ 151

F
Favorites
Bar (Explorer)......... 61
Center............... 62
Feeds
Button (Explorer)...... 64
Web.............. 60, 64
File
Explorer & Libraries... 35
History.............. 168
Menu bar options..... 40
File Explorer button...... 15
Finance App.......... 137
Firewall (Windows)..... 167
Folder
Create New... 37, 44, 109
Pane................ 72
Folders............... 28
Data................ 35
Mail................ 72
SkyDrive............. 47
System.............. 78
Food & Drink App...... 134
Full screen............ 24
Mode............... 101

G
Get
Directions............ 94
Help... 12, 132, 142, 170
Photos from camera.. 110
Go to button............ 67

Google................. 67
Grouping Internet tabs... 66

H
Hard Disc
Defragmenting....... 168
Management........ 167
Health & Fitness App... 133
Help
and Support......... 132
Button (Explorer).. 37, 43
Defender............ 170
Internet Explorer...... 69
Media Center........ 132
Option (File Explorer).. 40
Help+Tips App.......... 33
Hidden icons........... 19
Historical info (Weather) 141
History, browsing........ 63
Home
Button (Explorer)...... 57
Tab.............. 43, 44
HomeGroup.... 3, 117, 147
Sharing......... 117, 148
HTML code........... 101

I
Image (System)........ 169
Importing Photos....... 105
Inbox folder (Mail)....... 72
Information (System)... 163
InPrivate browsing....... 65
In-situ Upgrade.......... 2
Installation (clear)........ 2
Installing
Media Center........ 119
Programs........... 31
Windows 8.1.......... 2

Internet Explorer. 53
   Button. 15
   Help. 69
   Options. 53, 60
   Tabs. 16

J
Junk E-mail folder. 79

K
Key Statistics (Finance). 139
Keyboard (on-screen). . . 160

L
Lens View. 158
Libraries. 35, 45, 105
Library
   Folder. 117
   Locations. 45
Live Essentials. 4, 71
Locations
   Library. 45
   Recent. 39
   Search. 90
Lock Screen. 13
Looking after you PC. . . 163

M
Magnifier (Microsoft). . . . 158
Mail App. 71
   Attachment. 75
   Folders. 78
   Live. 71
Manage tab (Ribbon). . . . 44
Managing Print Jobs. 30
Manipulating windows. . . . 41
Map
   Address (People App). 84
   Navigation. 87, 100
   Views. 89

Maps App. 103
Market News. 137
Maximise button. 37, 41
Media
   Center. 128
   Player. 119
Menu bar options. 37, 39, 40
Menu bar (Bing). 60
Message Window. 73, 78, 84
Microsoft
   Magnifier. 158
   Narrator. 159
Minimise
   Button. 37
   Ribbon. 38, 43
Mobility Center. 150
Mouse
   Options. 161
   Pointers. 39
Moving window. 42
Music
   Library (Desktop). . . . 117
   Tools. 117

N
Narrator, Microsoft. 159
Navigating map area. 92
Navigation
   Bar (Bing). 87
   Buttons. 37, 39
   Controls (Bing maps). . 92
   Pane. . . . 36, 37, 124, 148
   Properties. 7
Nearby options (Maps). . . 90
Network
   Connection. 143, 145
   Icon. 19, 144
   Locations. 144
   Printer. 29
   Security. 146

Types. 19, 143
Wireless. 19, 143
New folder creation. . . 37, 44
News App. 135
Notification Area. . 15, 19, 30
Now Playing, Mode. 124

O
On-Screen keyboard. . . 160
Optimise hard disc. 167
Options
Button. 124
Display. 161
Key (Virtual keyboard) 160
Media Player. 127
Mouse. 161
Network connections. 144
Power. 151
Settings. 157, 163
Shut down. 20
Start menu. 6
Ordnance survey map. . . 89
Outbox folder (Mail). 72

P
Parts of window
File Explorer. 37
Player Library. 124
PC
Clock. 15, 19
Control. 26
Problem prevention. . 164
Settings. 25
System protection. . . . 168
People App. 81
Personalise PC. 22
Photo Viewer (Windows) 106
Photos App. 108
Photographs
Get from camera. 110

Print. 107
Scan. 112
Picture Tools. 37, 106
Pictures
Library. 75, 105
Tagging. 128, 144
Plans, Power. 151, 152
Playback controls. 126
Player
Library. 124, 126
View Modes. 124
Playing
DVDs. 128, 131
Videos. 116
Playlists. 126
Power
Button. 11, 19
Options. 151
Plans. 152
Preferences (Search). . . . 54
Prevention, Problem. . . . 164
Preview screen saver. . . . 24
Print
Button (Explorer). 61
Document. 30
Photos. 107
Jobs. 30
Maps. 97
Queue. 30
Printer
Configuring. 29
Control. 28
Default. 29, 113
Sharing. 149
Printing
Documents 30
E-mail messages. 79
Maps. 97
Problem prevention. 164
Product key. 129

Pro version, Windows 2, 119
Program
   Pin to Taskbar........ 16
   Run as Administrator. . 32
   Uninstall or Change. . . 31
Programs and Features. . 31
Protection, System..... 164
Public Transport........ 96

Q
Quick
   Access Help.......... 61
   Access Toolbar....... 43
   Accessibility panel... 156
   Search box.......... 37

R
Read Mail button (Explor.) 60
Read message window. . 78
Reading Pane (Mail)..... 72
Rearranging tiles........ 10
Receive attachment..... 77
Refresh button.......... 57
Rename
   Music folder........ 117
   Pictures............ 106
   Video.............. 115
Repair programs........ 31
Reply to E-mail message. 75
Requirements, System.... 3
Re-size window........ 41
Restart PC option....... 20
Restore
   Files............... 168
   System point........ 165
   Window button........ 38
Ribbon. 43, 37, 106, 117 155
Ripping from Audio CDs 123
Road map......... 99, 102

Router (Network)....... 144
Run as Administrator.... 32
Running Apps........... 17

S
Saver (screen)...... 23, 24
Scan
   Photos.............. 112
   Spyware............ 169
Screen
   Orientation.......... 151
   Resolution..... 3, 27, 151
   Savers.............. 24
Scroll bars............. 37
Search
   Box........ 39, 53, 55, 59
   Locations (Bing)...... 90
   Preferences (Bing).... 54
   Services (Bing)....... 91
   Web................ 55
Security.............. 166
   Wireless network..... 146
Send
   E-mail.............. 73
   Image by E-mail...... 76
Sent items folder....... 72
Server, Connecting to.... 71
Share tab (Ribbon)...... 44
Sharing
   Maps.............. 101
   Printer............. 149
Shut down options....... 20
Signal strength......... 145
Silverlight App......... 98
Sizing features (windows) 42
SkyDrive.............. 47
Sleep option... 20, 148, 154
Slide Show............ 106

Software
  Anti-spyware........ 169
  Anti-virus.............. 4
Spyware.............. 169
Start screen.......... 7, 14
Status
  Bar (Explorer)......... 58
  Buttons (Notification).. 19
Streetside view.......... 98
Synchronise..... 9, 49, 120
System
  Control............... 26
  Image.............. 169
  Information.......... 163
  Files.......... 164, 168
  Folders.............. 78
  Protection........... 164
  Requirements.......... 3
  Restore....... 164, 168
  Security............. 166
  Tray................ 19

T
Tabbed browsing........ 65
Tagging pictures....... 144
Taskbar bar........... 15
  Pinning to........ 18, 120
Test e-mail............. 73
Themes (Windows)...... 23
Thumbnail, Running Apps 16
Tile view.............. 10
Time, Change.......... 15
Tools button (Explorer)... 57
Traffic view........... 102
Turning off your PC...... 11
Types of network....... 143

U
Uninstall program....... 31
Update Windows....... 165

Upgrade via Windows 8... 2
Upload PDF (SkyDrive).. 52
URL.................. 56
USB devices.......... 154
User Accounts......... 21

V
Videos Library......... 115
View
  Modes (Player)...... 124
  Tab (Ribbon)......... 44
Viewer, Windows Photo. 106
Views Map (Bing)....... 87
Volume control..... 19, 151

W
Watchlist (Finance)..... 137
Weather App.......... 140
Web
  Feeds.............. 64
  Search.......... 53, 56
WEP security.......... 146
Window manipulation.... 42
Windows
  Calendar............. 85
  Defender........... 169
  Desktop.......... 7, 10
  Environment.......... 13
  Firewall............. 167
  Key (keyboard).... 15, 155
  Live account.......... 4
  Media Center........ 128
  Media Player........ 119
  Mobility Center....... 150
  Music App........... 118
  Photo viewer........ 106
  Power plans......... 152
  Scan facility......... 112
  Screens............. 13
  Settings charm....... 11

Themes............. 23
Video App........... 116
Wi-Fi................ 143
Wireless
    Network............ 143
    Network security..... 146
    Router............. 143
Working with Programs. . 31
WPA security......... 146

X
Xbox Player.......... 118

Z
Zipping Files to SkyDrive. 50
Zoom link (Bing)........ 88
Zooming in or out...... 172